# Progressive

# BLUES
# RHYTHM
# GUITAR
# METHOD

## by

## Peter Gelling

**Acknowledgements**
Cover Photograph: Phil Martin
Photographs: Phil Martin


Distributed by:

**Koala Publications Pty. Ltd.**
37 Orsmond Street Hindmarsh,
South Australia 5007
AUSTRALIA
Ph: 61-8-8346 5366
Fax: 61-8-8340 9033
Email: info@koalapub.com.au
or visit our web page at:
www.koalapub.com.au


**I.S.B.N. 1 864690 59 3**
**Order Codes:**

| Book | 69059 |
| CD Pack | CP-69059 |
| CD Only | CD-69059 |

# Contents

## SECTION 1             11
### Basic Blues Chords and Progressions

## SECTION 2             27
### Moveable Chords

4

## SECTION 3      49
**Single Note Riffs, Boogie Rhythms**

## SECTION 4      67
**Shuffles, Turnarounds**

# Introduction

This book takes an innovative approach to learning Blues rhythm guitar. *Progressive Blues Rhythm Guitar Method* uses both chords and single note riffs to help the student gain control of timing and rhythms, which are essential in creating good rhythm parts. The book contains a study of both open and moveable chords, before moving on to single and double note riffs which include many of the classic Blues sounds.

The method uses five basic major chord shapes and shows how many other chords can be derived from them and moved to every key. The book also contains an in depth study of dominant 7th chords, which are the heart of the Blues sound. A variety of chord forms are introduced within a framework that quickly allows the student to play confidently over the entire fretboard. Other essential sounds such as the 9th chord are also introduced. Exercises are introduced in a progressive manner, encouraging the development of both hands.

In Blues playing what you do with the notes and where you put them is much more important than how many different notes you play. It is largely the phrasing and timing, along with imaginative use of rhythms that distinguishes the great players from the rest. This book presents a study of note and rest values along with ties and expressive rhythm techniques such as staccato and percussive strumming, along with an explanation of different feels such as straight or swing 8ths and the shuffle.

By the end of the book, the student will be playing authentic Blues rhythm parts as played by the greats.

To improve your skills even further it is recommended that you use a metronome or drum machine with all the examples in the book. It would also be helpful to play along with the recording that accompanies the book. If you are serious about music, a good teacher can often help you progress much quicker than you can on your own.

# Using the Compact Disc

It is recommended that you have a copy of the accompanying compact disc that includes all the examples in this book. The book shows you where to put your fingers and what technique to use and the recording lets you hear how each example should sound. Practice the examples slowly at first, gradually increasing tempo. Once you are confident you can play the example evenly without stopping the beat, try playing along with the recording. You will hear a drum beat at the beginning of each example, to lead you into the example and to help you keep time. A small diagram of a compact disc with a number as shown below indicates a recorded example. Some of the tracks on the CD contain more than one example. In these cases, index points are used (1.0, 1.1, 1.2 etc). If your CD player has an index points function, you can select each example individually. If not, each example will automatically follow the previous one. The first track on the CD contains the notes of the six open strings of the guitar. 1.0 is the open 6th string (low E note), 1.1 is the open A string, 1.2 is the open D string, etc.

**1.0** ← CD Track Number

# Chord Diagrams

Chords are learnt with the help of a **chord diagram**. This will show you exactly where to place your left hand fingers in order to play a particular chord. A chord diagram is a grid of horizontal and vertical lines representing the strings and frets of the guitar as shown below.

## Left Hand Fingering

**1** Index Finger

**2** Middle Finger

**3** Ring Finger

**4** Little Finger

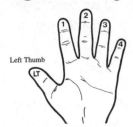

Left Thumb

**E** ← Chord Symbol

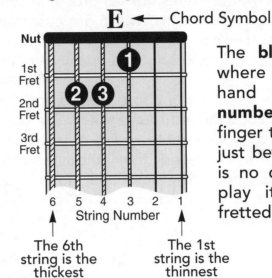

The **black dots** show you where to place your left hand fingers. The **white number** tells you which finger to place on the string just before the fret. If there is no dot on a string, you play it as an open (not fretted) string.

The other chord diagram symbols used in this book are summarised with the following two chord shapes.

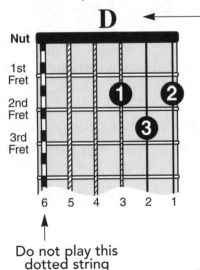

Do not play this dotted string

Chord symbol for **D** chord.

A **dotted** string indicates that string is not to be strummed. An **X** on the string indicates that string is to be **dampened** by another finger lightly touching it. The string is still strummed as a part of the chord but it is not heard.

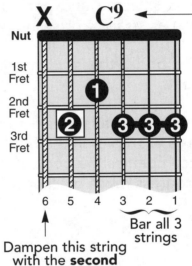

Dampen this string with the **second finger** by lightly touching it.

Chord symbol for **C ninth** chord.

A small **bar** connecting several black dots indicates they are held down by the same finger. This is called **barring.**

**2** = Key Note

# Easy Read Rhythm Notation

Many strumming rhythms are shown in the course of the book, wherever tablature is not used. If you are not able to read music, use the Easy Read notation. This system will show you which chord must be fretted (indicated above the Easy Read boxes) and which type of strum must be used (shown inside the Easy Read Boxes). The correct rhythm count is also shown.

**Chord to be fretted**

**Strumming Arrows**

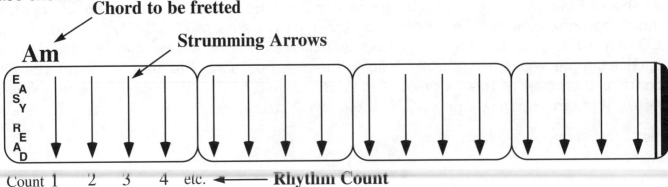

Count 1    2    3    4   etc. ← **Rhythm Count**

# Fretboard Diagrams

Fretboard diagrams are given throughout this book to show which patterns and fingerings are given for each scale. To know how to read the diagrams, study the following illustration.

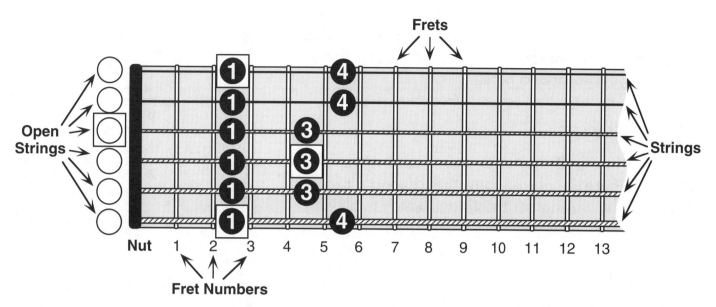

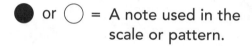 = A note used in the scale or pattern.

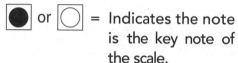 = Indicates the note is the key note of the scale.

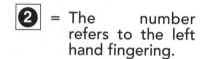 = The number refers to the left hand fingering.

## Left Hand Fingering

**1** Index Finger
**2** Middle Finger
**3** Ring Finger
**4** Little Finger

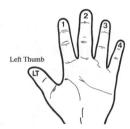

# Tablature

This book uses standard music notation and tablature notation. If you cannot read music notes, use the tab written below the music. Music readers will need to look at the tab to see what technique is being used to play certain notes (e.g. hammer-on, slide etc).

**Tablature** is a method of indicating the position of notes on the fretboard. There are six "tab" lines each representing one of the six strings on the guitar.

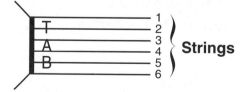

When a number is placed on one of the lines, it indicates the fret location of the note e.g.

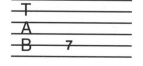

This indicates the **seventh** fret of the **5th** string (an **E** note).

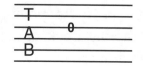

This indicates the **3rd** string open (a **G** note).

# Tablature Symbols

The following tablature symbols are used throughout this book.

## The Hammer-On

A curved line and the letter H indicates a hammer. The first note is played but the second note is produced by hammering on the left hand finger which plays the second note.

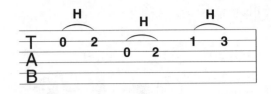

## The Pull-Off

A curved line and the letter P indicates a pull-off. The first note is played but the second note is produced by pulling off the finger which is playing the first note.

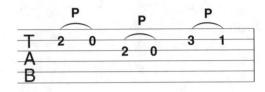

## The Slide

The letter S and a straight line represents a slide. If the line comes from below the number, slide from a lower fret but if the line is above the number, slide from a higher fret. The third example on the right shows the desired fret to slide from.

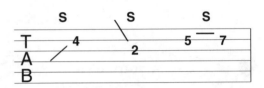

## The Bend

The letter B and a curved arrow represents a bend. The note is played by the left hand finger which bends the string (from the note indicated in the tab.

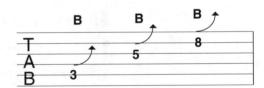

## The Release Bend

A curved arrow on the top left hand side of the number and the letter R indicates a release bend. This technique involves bending the note indicated with the left hand, plucking the string whilst bent, then returning the string to its normal position. The release bend creates a drop in pitch from a higher note to a lower note.

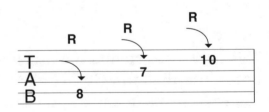

## Vibrato

A wavy line shown above the tablature indicates when vibrato is used. Vibrato is controlled with the left hand finger which is fretting the note. As the finger frets the note move the finger rapidly back and forth in the direction of the adjacent strings.

# Technique

## Right Hand Technique

### Picking Grip

The traditional picking grip is holding the pick with the thumb and the last joint of the first finger. There are variations on this grip but I recommend trying this method, as it will prove more efficient in most applications.

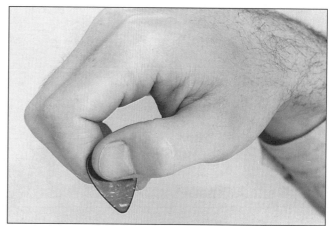

*Hold pick with thumb and first finger.*

## Right Hand Position

There are basically two right hand positions when using the pick. The first is closing the fingers of the right hand, and the second position is opening the hand across the face of the guitar. Try both positions and decide which one you are most comfortable with.

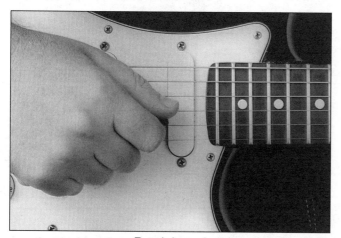

*Position 1*

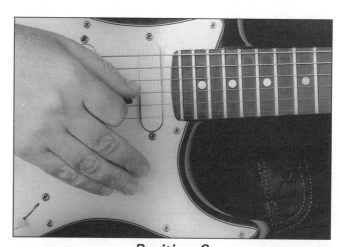

*Position 2*

To assist with keeping the right hand steady when picking, try bracing the fourth finger on the face of the guitar as shown in the accompanying photo. This position is particularly helpful in picking situations but is not used when strumming.

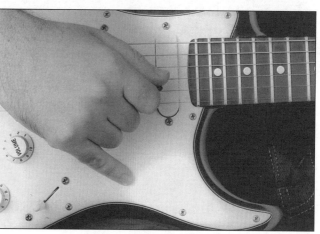

*Brace fourth finger*

# Left Hand Technique

All notes must be fretted with the tips of the fingers and positioned as close as practical to the fretwires.

*Fingertips as close as practical to fretwires.*

## Left Hand Position

There are basically two positions for the left hand. In most cases the left hand thumb should be positioned behind the neck of the guitar with the fingers evenly arched over the fretboard.

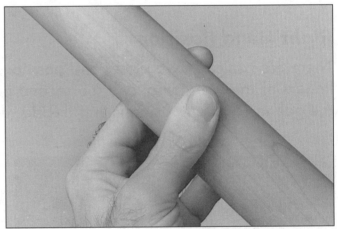

*Thumb positioned behind neck.*

When using techniques such as the bend, release bend, vibrato etc. you may find it more comfortable to have the left hand thumb in a higher position, wrapped over the top of the fretboard.

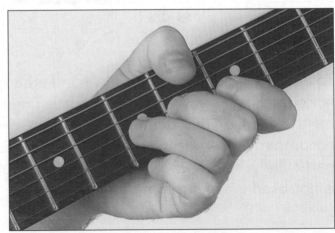

*Thumb positioned over the neck.*

# SECTION 1

# Basic Blues Chords, Blues Progressions

# LESSON ONE
## Basic Chords

A **chord** is a group of three or more notes played together. Most chords are derived from a **Major Scale**. Here is the C Major scale.

 **2.0**

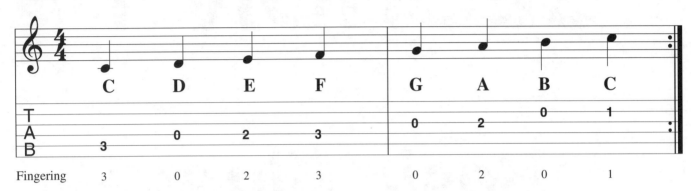

This next example contains a **C Major chord**. The major chord is obtained by taking the **1st**, **3rd** and **5th** degrees of the scale and playing them together. Any major chord is usually described by its letter name only, so a C major chord would usually be called a C chord.

 **2.1**

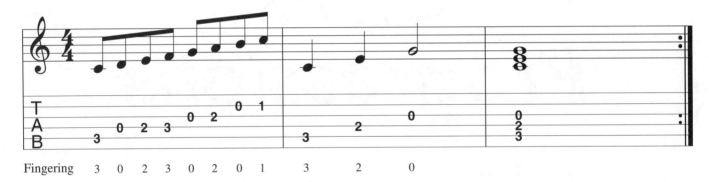

Here is the most common fingering for a C chord. Although this chord contains more than three notes, there are still only three different notes. C and E occur twice in this fingering. Doubling notes is very common in guitar chords.

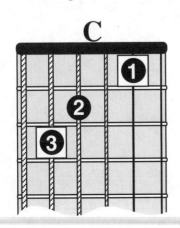

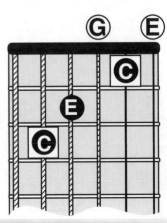

Try strumming the C chord as shown in Example 3.0. If you have never read rhythms before, follow the easy read arrows which indicate downstrokes only in this exercise. Be sure to count and try tapping your foot on each of the beats as you play.

 **3.0**

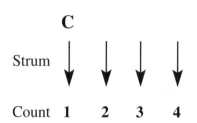

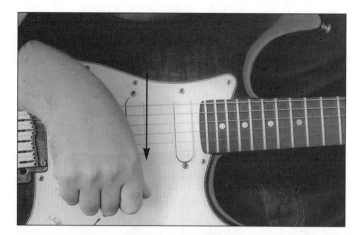

*The Down Strum*

# Chord Progressions

## Staff

A standard music staff will be used to show you which chords have to be played and how long a certain chord must be played for. The music staff consists of five lines with a treble clef at the beginning of the staff.

## Bars

The staff is divided into sections called bars or measures. The bars are separated by a vertical line called a bar line with a double bar line to mark the end of a progression. There are four "beats" or four "counts" to every bar as indicated by the time signature at the beginning of the staff. At this stage you will strum one down-strum on every beat of the bar. Example 3.1 shows a C Major chord being strummed for four bars.

 **3.1**

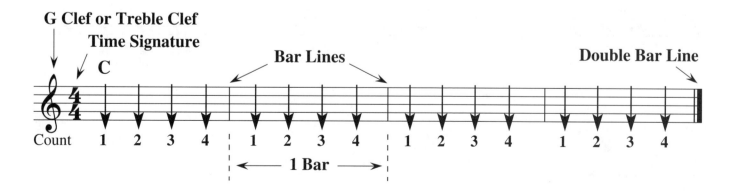

# LESSON TWO

## 12 Bar Blues

Here are two new chords to practice, **F** and **G**. Memorise the fingering for each chord and then try moving from one to the other. Also practice moving from C to F and C to G. Once you can do this you should be ready for Example 4 which is a **12 Bar Blues** progression.

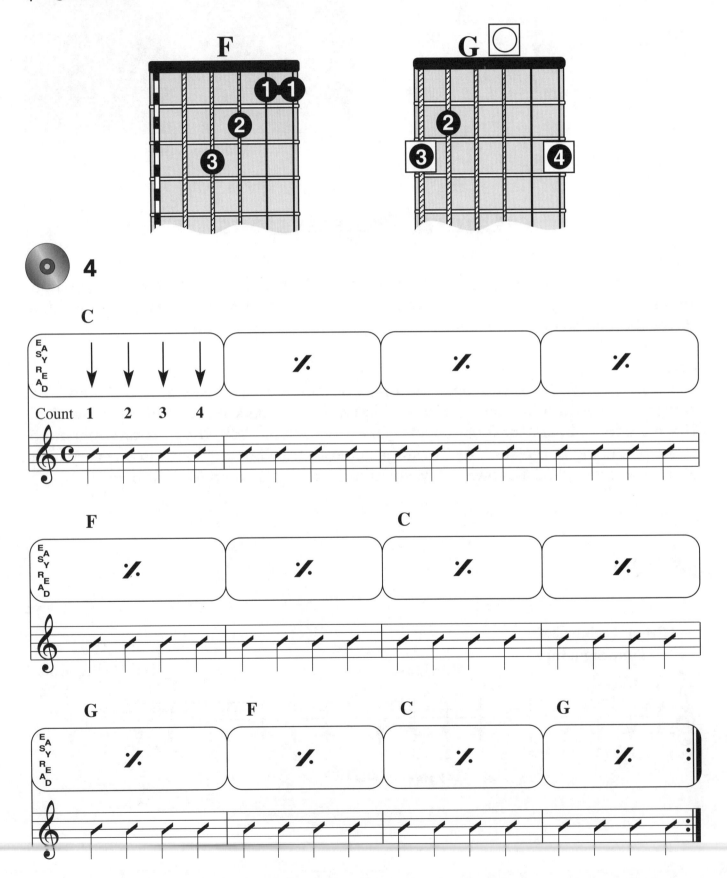

Since the 12 Bar Blues is the most common progression in Blues music, it is worth looking at it in more detail. There are usually three different chords used. Each of these chords relates to one basic **Key.** The key is the central note around which a piece of music is based. For example, a piece of music in the key of C would be made up of notes from the C major scale. Chords can be built from any notes of the scale. In Blues, the most common chords are those built on notes **1**, **4** and **5** of the major scale. So in the key of C, these chords would be **C**, **F** and **G**.

# C Major Scale

C D E F G A B C
1 2 3 4 5 6 7 8(1)

Chord numbers in music are usually indicated by roman numerals, as shown below.

**C    F    G**

**I̲    I̲V̲    V̲**

Here is the 12 bar Blues progression again, this time shown in roman numerals.

Although there will be variations later in the book, the basic order of chords in a 12 bar Blues is – **Chord I̲** (first four bars), **Chord I̲V̲** (bars 5 and 6), back to **Chord I̲** (bars 7 and 8), **Chord V̲** (bar 9), **Chord I̲V̲** (bar 10), **Chord I̲** (bar 11) and **Chord V̲** for the final bar (bar 12).

A good way to memorise the progression is to visualise it bar by bar. Study the progression shown above until you think you have it memorised. Then shut the book and try asking yourself questions like... what chord is in bar 6? (Answer- I̲V̲). What chord is in bar 9? (V̲), Bar 3? (I̲) etc until you can answer instantly.

# LESSON THREE

## Key of G

In the key of G, chords I, IV and V will come from the G major scale as shown below.

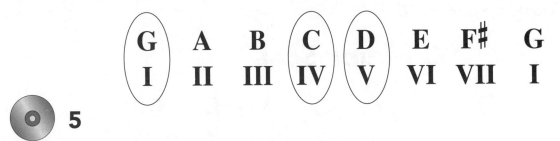

**5**

Fingaring    0    2    0    1      3    0    2     3

The new chord here is **D**. Memorise the fingering and then practice changing between **D** and **G** and also **D** and **C**.

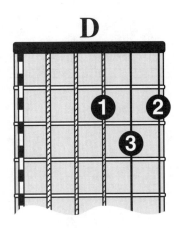

Now try Example 6 for an idea of how these three chords sound when used in the key of G.

**6**

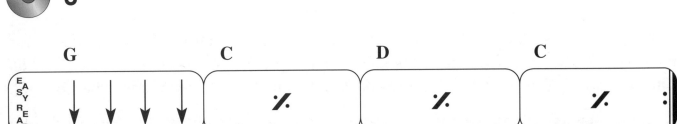

# The Up-Strum

Up to this point, only downstrokes of the pick have been used. This works well when strumming on the beat, but for extra strums between the beats it is often necessary to use upstrokes, or up-strums. A good way to get used to up-strums is to set up a pattern of constant down and up strumming, counting **1 and 2 and three and 4 and** as you go. Try to keep your strumming smooth and even. The symbol **+** is often used in place of the word **and.**

**7**

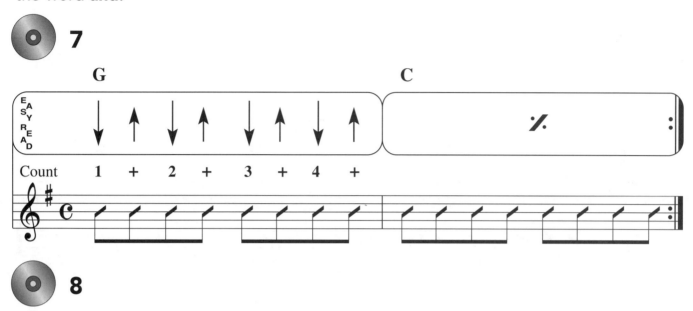

Here is a 12 bar Blues in the key of G using a variation on the constant strumming pattern. Remember to tap your foot on the beat and count as you play.

**8**

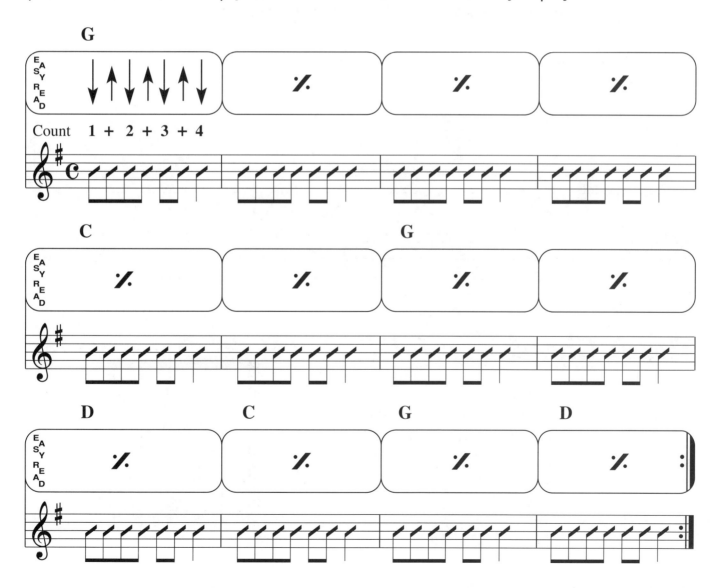

# LESSON FOUR

## New Strumming Patterns, Key of D

Once you have control of strumming down and up, try experimenting with different patterns by putting up-strums in between only some of the beats. Here are some examples.

 9

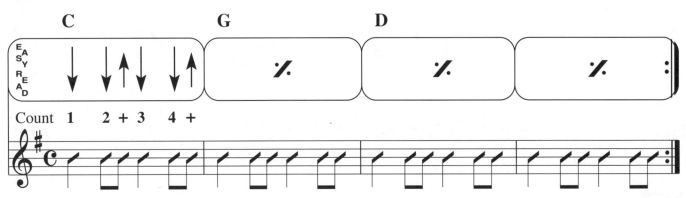

The next thing to try is leaving out one or more of the down-strums. This means you will not be playing on some of the beats where your foot is tapping. This creates an effect known as **syncopation.** Here is an example. Practice it slowly at first.

 10.0

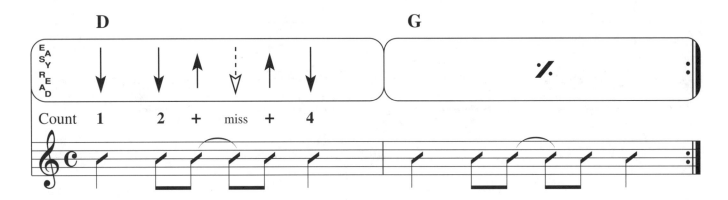

## The A Chord

Another common open position chord is **A**. Memorise the fingering and then practice changing between **A** and **D** and also **A** and **G**.

# Key of D

Here are the notes of the D major scale. Once again, notes I, IV and V are the most important for now because the chords for a 12 bar Blues in the key of D will be built on them.

Chord V in this key is a new one ... **A**. Practice changing between **A** and **G** as well as **A** and **D** as shown in Example 10.1 Then play a 12 bar Blues in the key of D.

**10.1**

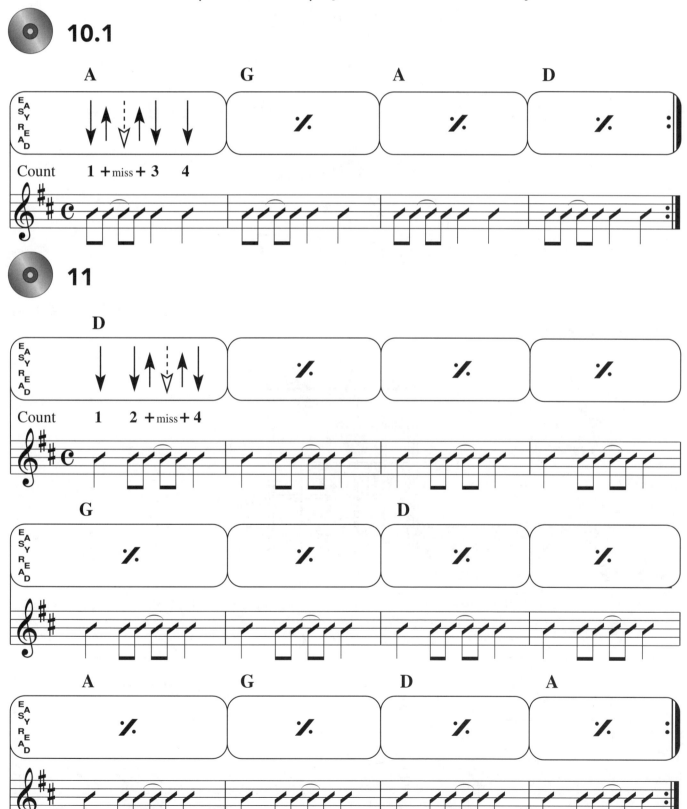

# LESSON FIVE

## 7th Chords

One of the most common sounds in Blues is the **Dominant 7th** chord, (commonly called a 7th chord. Like the major chord, 7th chords can be derived from the major scale. A 7th chord is obtained by adding the flattened 7th degree (note) of the scale to a major chord.

## C Major Scale

| C | D | E | F | G | A | B | C |
|---|---|---|---|---|---|---|---|
| 1 | 2 | 3 | 4 | 5 | 6 | 7 | 8 |

## C7 Chord

| C | E | G | B♭ |
|---|---|---|-----|
| 1 | 3 | 5 | ♭7 |

Here is a common fingering for a C7 chord. Practice changing between **C** and **C7** as shown in Example 12.

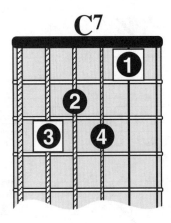

**12**

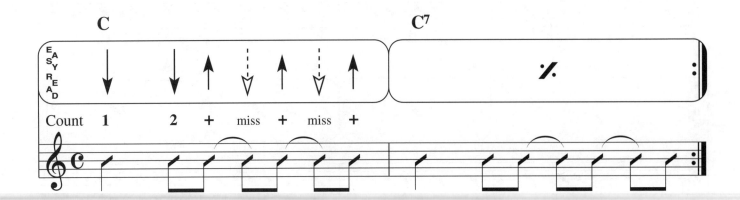

It is possible to build a 7th chord from any basic major chord. Here are some new ones to learn.

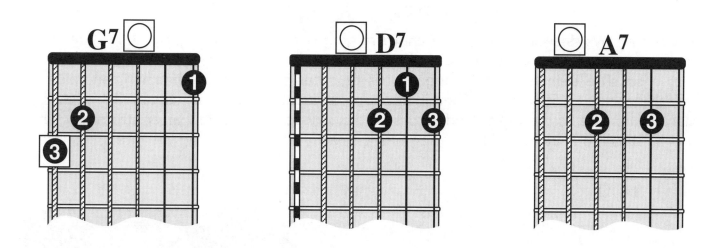

# Chord Charts

Practice changing between these chords in various combinations, then play Example 13 which is written in the form of a chord chart such as one you might find in a songbook. Once you know the right chord shapes, you can interpret a chord chart easily and make any progression sound good. The chart here shows one strum per beat, but you could use any of the strums you have learnt as well as making up some of your own.

 **13**

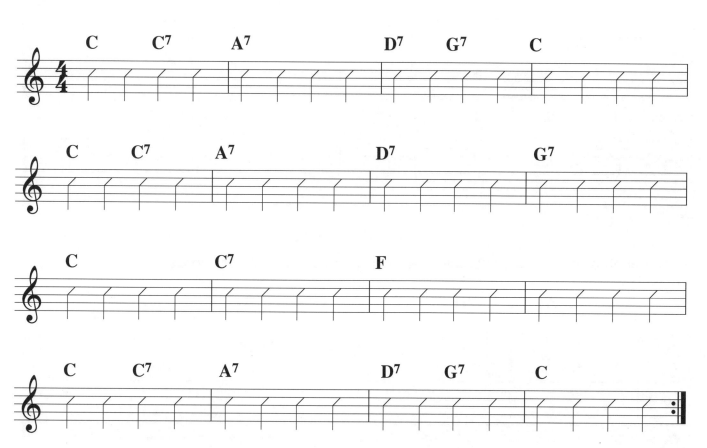

# LESSON SIX

## Staccato, Key of A

It is not always desirable to leave a chord ringing once it has been played. In Blues it is common to cut the sound of a chord off as soon as it has been played, making the rhythm very crisp. The technique of cutting chords or notes shorter than their written value is called staccato. With chords containing open strings, staccato is usually achieved by placing the side of the right hand across all the strings immediately after strumming the chord. Staccato is indicated by placing a dot directly above or below the intended note.

**14.0**

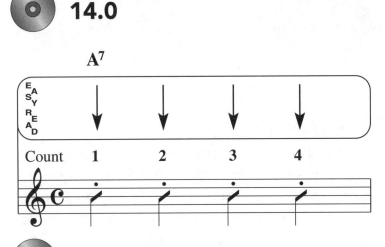

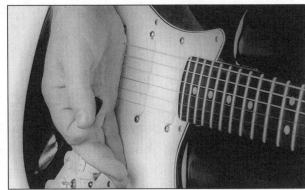

*Place right hand across strings after strum.*

**14.1**

This one uses staccato on the second and fourth beats of each bar. You may have heard this sound used in early Jazz songs.

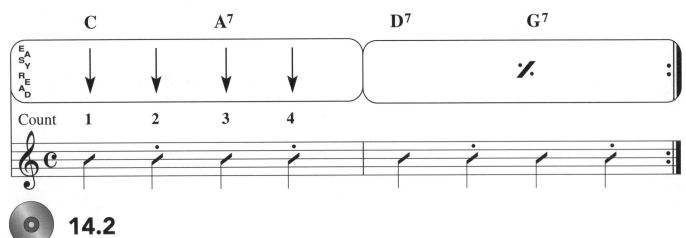

**14.2**

Here's another one to practice, this time changing between major chords and 7th chords.

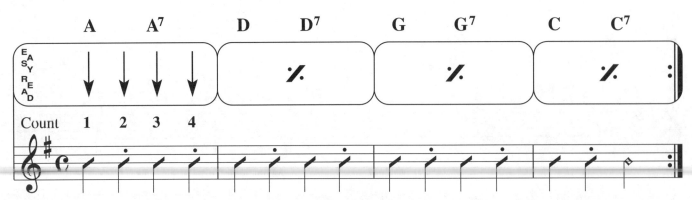

# Key of A

In the key of **A**, chords $\bar{\text{I}}$, $\bar{\text{IV}}$ and $\bar{\text{V}}$ will come from the A major scale.

Chord V here is an **E chord**, which may also be extended to become **E7**. Here are common fingerings for both these chords.

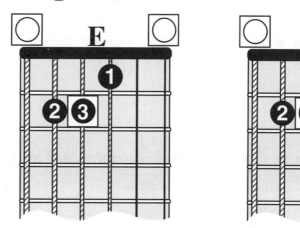

 **15**

In Blues it is common to use 7ths for all the chords. This 12 bar Blues in the key of A uses a combination of major chords and 7th chords. Notice how the 7ths make this one sound more bluesy than the previous exercises using only major chords. The staccato technique is used once again, this time with a slightly different strumming pattern.

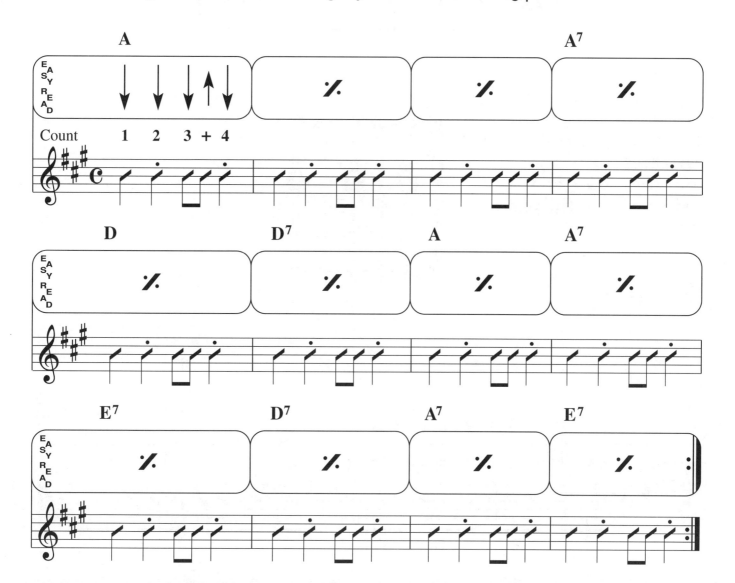

# LESSON SEVEN

## Triplets, Key of E

One of the most important rhythms in Blues is the triplet. A triplet is a group of three notes spaced evenly across a beat. A good way to count triplets is to count the number for each beat and then break up the word triplet for the remaining two parts of the beat. A bar of 4/4 time would be counted... One trip-let, Two trip-let, Three trip-let, Four trip-let. There are several ways of strumming triplets, but for now it is best to use all downstrokes.

 **16.0**

Notice how each of the triplets has the number 3 in the middle.

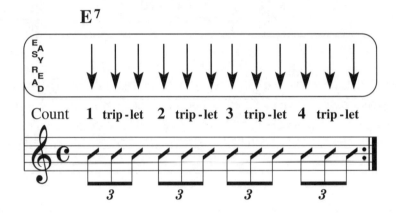

This next one contains a new chord ... **B7**. Play this one very slowly at first and be sure to tap your foot and count.

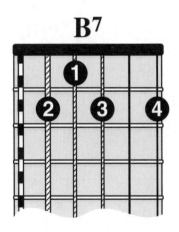

 **16.1**

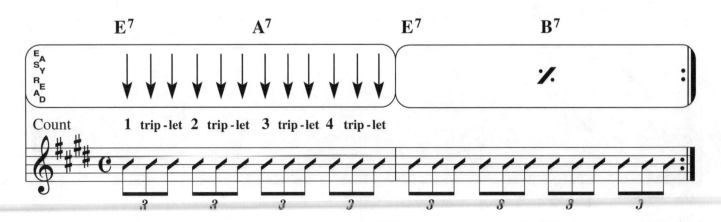

# Key of E

Continuing on with the study of different keys, here are the notes for the E major scale. Chords I, IV and V will now be E or E7, A or A7 and B or B7.

| E | F♯ | G♯ | A | B | C♯ | D♯ |
|---|----|----|----|----|----|----|
| I | II | III | IV | V | VI | VII |

Here is a 12 bar Blues in E using a constant triplet rhythm. Once you play the progression with this rhythm added to the sound of 7th chords, it really starts to sound like Blues.

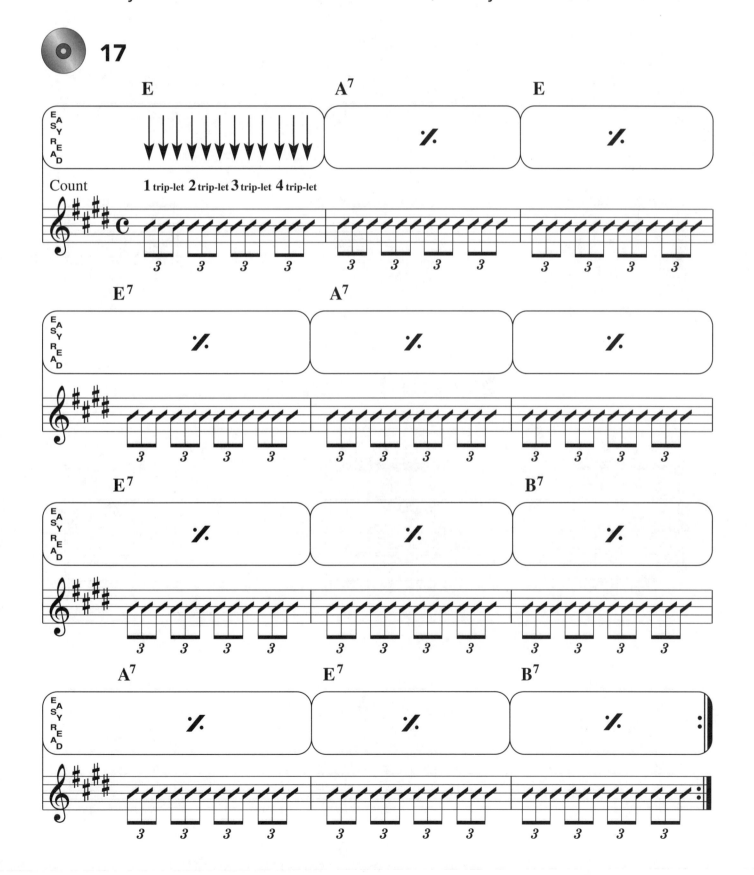

# Summary of Chords

Here is a summary of all the chords presented in Section 1. Section 2 contains all new chords, many of them based on the shapes on this page. Make sure you are quite comfortable with all of them before moving on.

## *Major Chords*

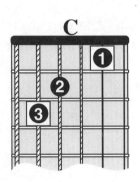
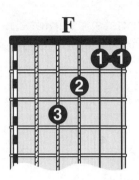
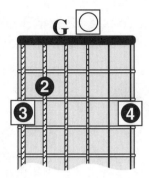

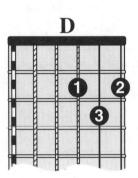
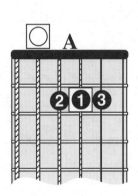
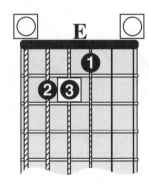

## *Seventh Chords*

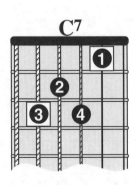
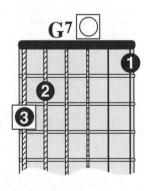
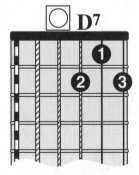

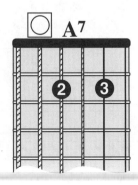
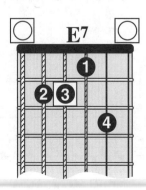
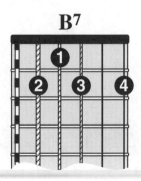

# SECTION 2

# Moveable Chords

# LESSON EIGHT

# The Bar Chord

All the chords studied in Section 1 were "open chords"; i.e. they contain at least one open string. In this lesson the "bar chord" is introduced. The term bar chord means that the first finger **bars** across all the strings. The fact that there are no open strings in a bar chord means it is possible to move the one shape to all positions of the fretboard and play in every key.

## Root Six Major Bar Chord

The first bar chord you will learn is the "Root Six Major" bar chord, meaning two things. Firstly the term "Root Six" indicates that the root of the chord or the name of the chord is found on the sixth string. Secondly, the word "Major" points out exactly what type of chord it is.

The Root Six Major bar chord is based upon the basic E Major chord and can be learnt in three steps.

## Step One

Finger the basic E Major chord with the second, third and fourth fingers, therefore leaving the first finger free.

## Step Two

Now move this fingering of the basic E Major chord up the fretboard one whole fret.

## Step Three

Finally, lay the first finger across the fret thus barring all the strings (as indicated by a curved line). By doing this your first finger is doing the same job as the nut except one fret higher. This completes the raising of the basic E Major chord one fret. A new chord, F Major, is produced because the F note (or F chord) is always found one fret higher than E. As mentioned above, the root note (F) is found on the sixth string. The root note will be highlighted by a box.

**F**

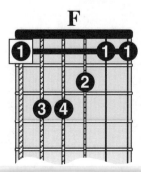 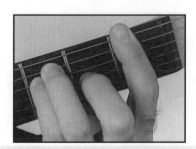

# Left Hand Technique

Bar chords are very difficult to play at first and will require a great deal of practice before they are comfortable to use. Try to keep the first finger of the left hand straight and parallel to the fret wires. It is also important to keep the other fingers arched and use the tips of the fingers only. The left hand thumb must be kept behind the neck.

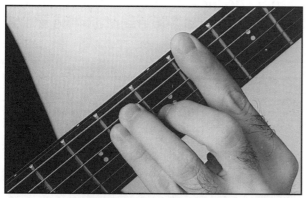

*Keep first finger straight.*

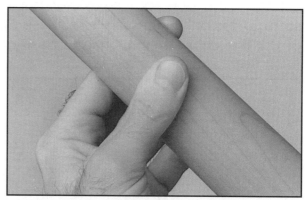

*Keep thumb behind neck.*

# Notes on the Sixth String

The Root Six Major bar chord can be played at any fret though the name of the chord will depend on which note the first finger is fretting on the sixth string. In order to determine exactly where a certain chord must be played it will be necessary to know the notes on the sixth string. The diagram below illustrates the notes on the sixth string and gives three examples of the Root Six Major bar chord.

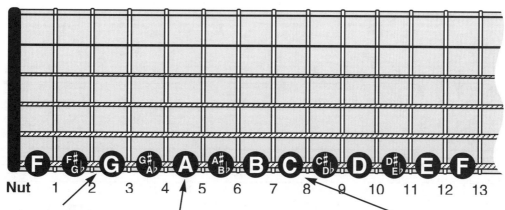

In order to play a G Major bar chord, position the root six Major bar chord on the 3rd fret.

In order to play an A Major bar chord, position the root six Major bar chord on the 5th fret.

In order to play a C Major bar chord, position the root six Major bar chord on the 8th fret.

| G | A | C |
|---|---|---|

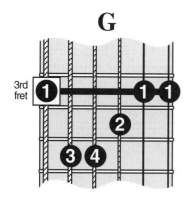
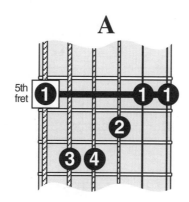
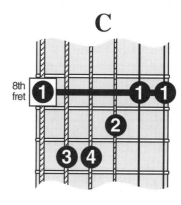

# LESSON NINE

## Bar Chord Blues

Once you can make a bar chord sound reasonably good in several positions on the fretboard, the next step is to learn to change positions smoothly and in time. As you change from one root six Major bar chord to another, do not lift your fingers off the strings. It is only necessary to release the pressure in the left hand and maintain the shape of the bar chord as you change positions.

*Release pressure in left hand.*

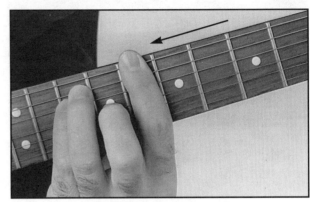

*Maintain chord shape and
slide to next position.*

 **18.0**

Practice changing between chords very slowly at first.

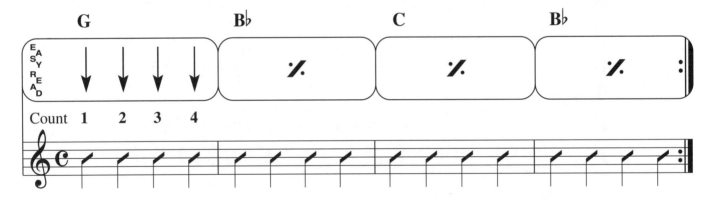

 **18.1**

The better you know the notes on the 6th string, the easier it will be to play all root 6 bar chord progressions.

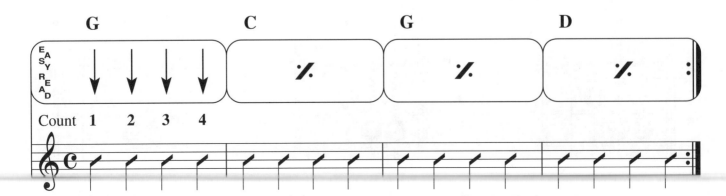

**19**

Here is a 12 bar Blues in the key of C, using only root 6 bar chords. This progression contains a common blues variation, moving to chord IV (F) in the second bar. This is often referred to as a **Quick IV**. In this exercise it will be necessary to move down the neck to chords IV and V instead of up. Notice the use of constant triplets as the rhythm once again. Try to keep your wrist loose as you strum and remember to use all downstrokes.

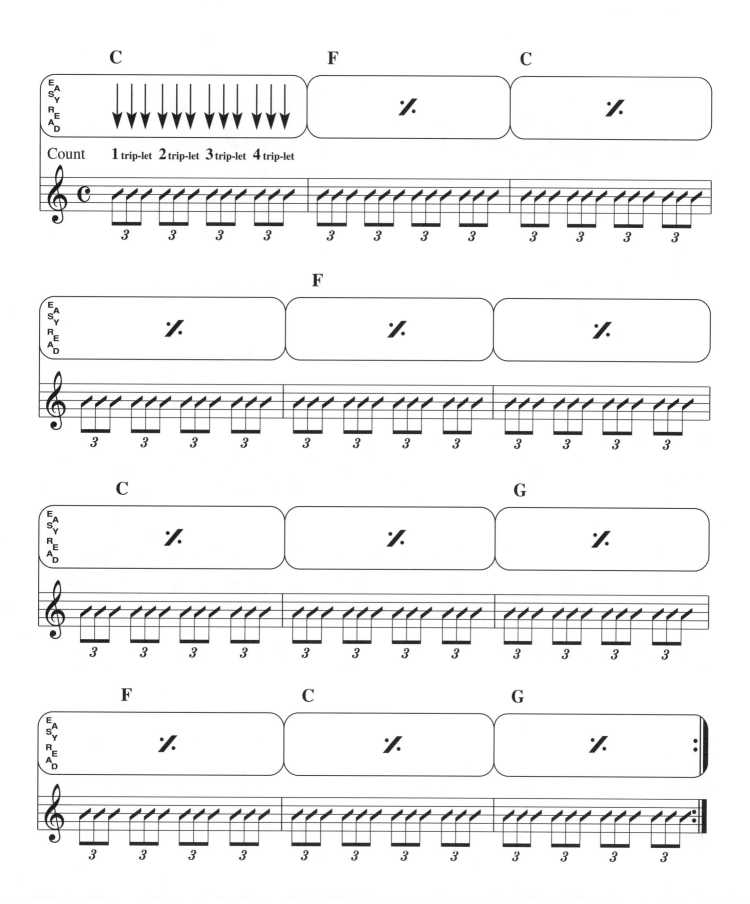

# LESSON TEN

# *7th Bar Chords, Rhythm Techniques*

Probably more important for Blues than the major bar chord is the root 6 bar chord 7th. It can be thought of as a variation on the root 6 major bar chord shape. The only difference is that the little finger is placed one fret further up the neck on the second string. Like the major bar chord, the shape remains the same regardless of the position on the fretboard.

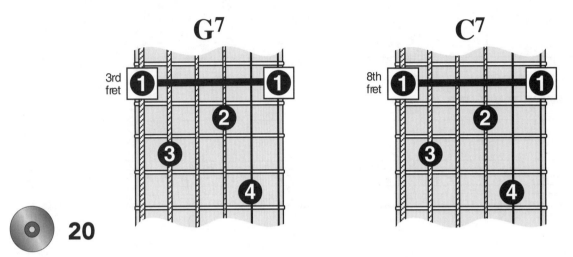

**20**

Practice changing between the major bar chord and the 7th bar chord, then try this 12 bar Blues which makes use of both.

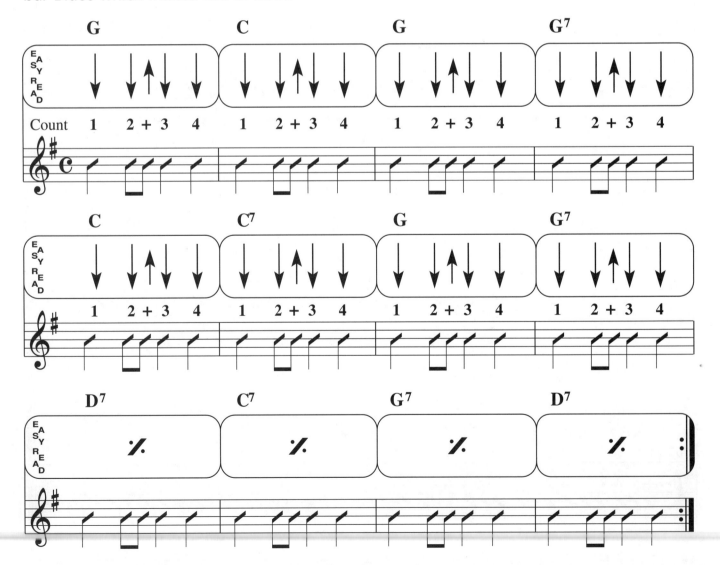

# Staccato

With open chords, staccato is performed with the right hand. However, when using bar chords it is achieved by lifting the left hand fingers off the fretboard (but not completely off the strings) as soon as the chord has been played. Here are two examples.

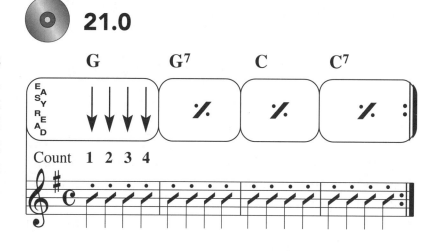

## Percussive Strumming

Another important rhythm technique is the use of the **Percussive Strum**. It is achieved by forming a chord shape with the left hand and placing it on the strings, but **not** pressed down on the frets. A percussive strum is indicated by using an **X** in place of a notehead. Listen to the accompanying record-ing to hear what the percussive strum should sound like. Example 21.2 alternates between a chord played normally, and percussive strumming.

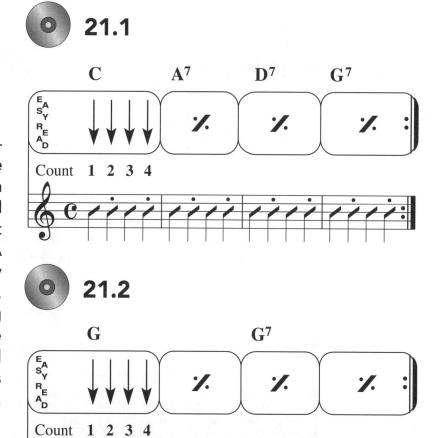

 **21.3**

This one demonstrates the use of both staccato and percussive strumming. The use of these techniques really helps to drive the rhythm along.

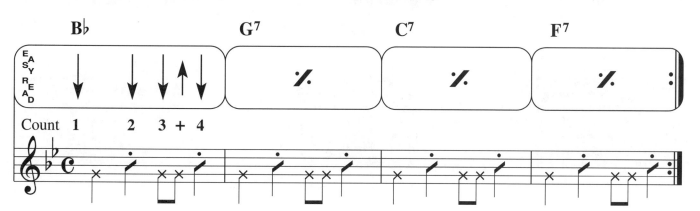

# LESSON ELEVEN

## Root 5 Bar Chords

As the term root 5 suggests, the root (name) of these chords can be determined from the note on the fifth string, fretted with the first finger bar. Like all bar chords, the same shape can be moved up or down to any position on the fretboard. Below is the basic shape for the root 5 Major bar chord shown in two positions. You will need to have patience with this chord shape, as the combination of the first finger bar and the partial bar with the third finger is particularly difficult at first. Make sure the third finger sounds the 4th, 3rd and 2nd strings, but **not** the 1st string.

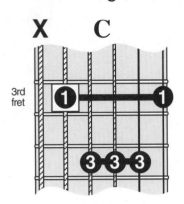
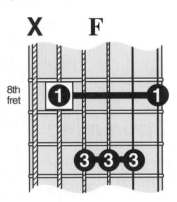

It will be necessary to know the notes on the fifth string in order to know on which fret a root 5 chord must be fretted. The diagram below illustrates all notes on the fifth string up to the 13th fret. Try naming a chord and moving to the correct fret. Practice this until you can do it instantly.

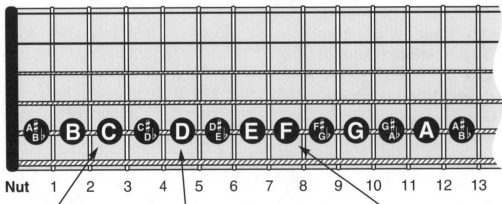

In order to play a C Major bar chord, position the root five Major bar chord on the 3rd fret.

In order to play an D Major bar chord, position the root five Major bar chord on the 5th fret.

In order to play a F Major bar chord, position the root five Major bar chord on the 8th fret.

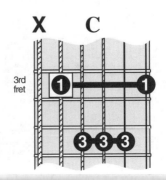
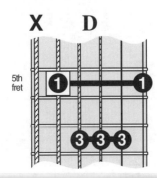
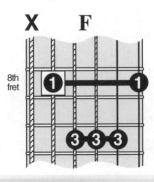

# Root 5 Seventh Chords

After learning the root 5 major chord, it is important to also know how to play 7th chords as root 5 chords. Here is the basic shape. Once again, have patience with this one as it can be difficult to control at first.

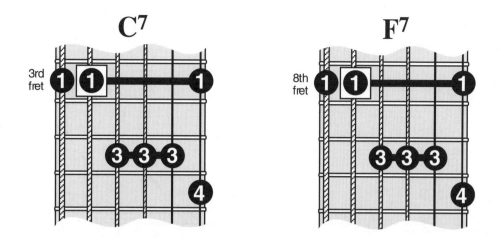

 **22**

Here is a 12 bar Blues using root 5 major and root 5 seventh chords.

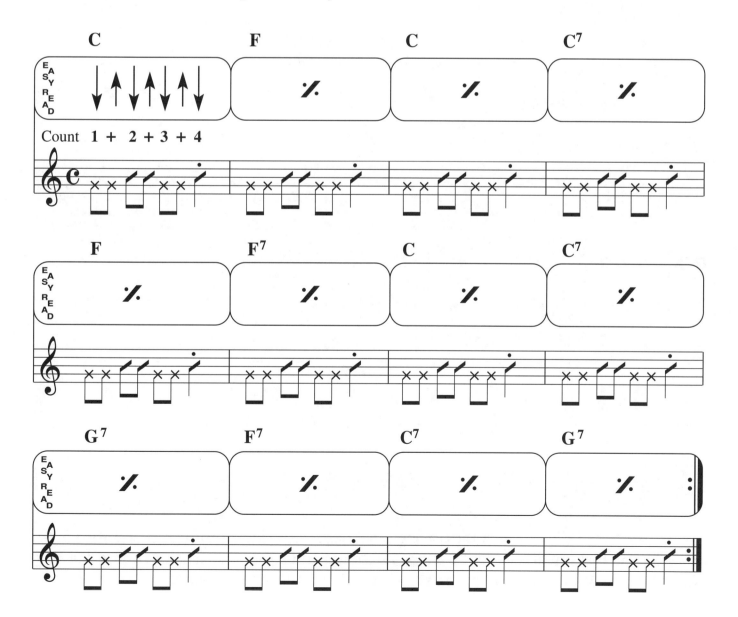

# LESSON TWELVE

## Changing Between Shapes

Once you know how to play both root 6 and root 5 bar chords, the next step is learning how to combine them. Here are a couple of exercises to help you gain control of changing between the two major bar chords.

**23.0**

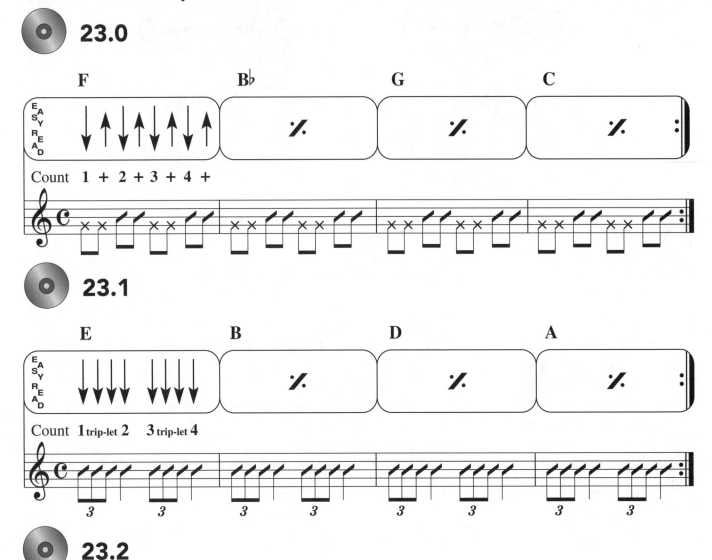

**23.1**

**23.2**

Now try this one featuring the two 7th chord shapes.

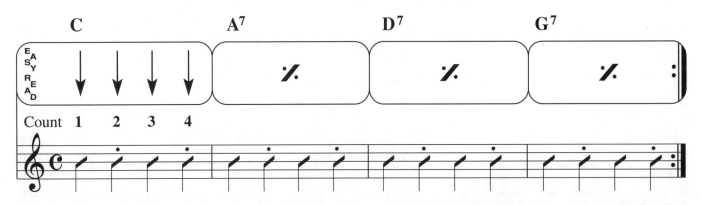

There are two basic patterns for playing a 12 barBlues using both root 6 and root 5 bar chords. The first one uses a root 6 shape as chord $\overline{\text{I}}$ and a root 5 shape for chords $\overline{\text{IV}}$ and $\overline{\text{V}}$. Chords $\overline{\text{I}}$ and $\overline{\text{IV}}$ will be found at the same fret, chord $\overline{\text{V}}$ will be up two frets.

**24**

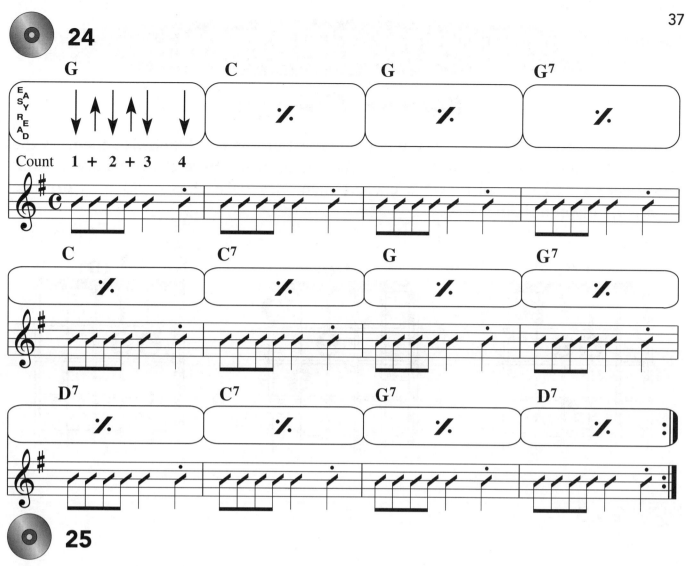

**25**

Here is the second pattern. This time Chord $\underline{I}$ will be root 5. Chord $\underline{V}$ will be root 6 at the same fret, while chord $\underline{IV}$ will be root 6 down two frets.

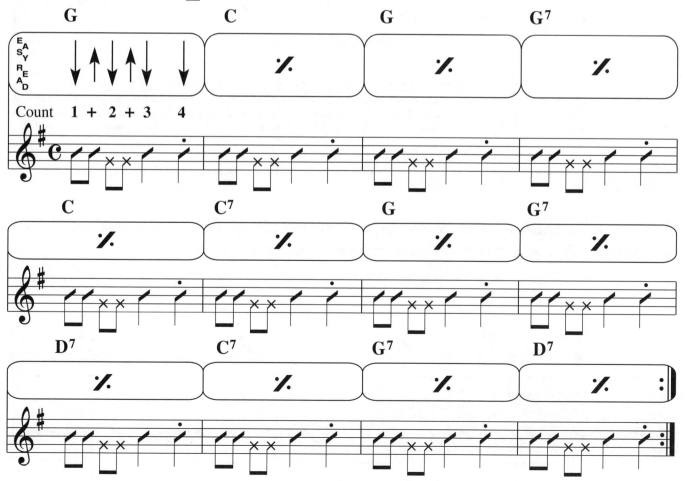

# LESSON THIRTEEN

## Minor Chords

Open minor chords are not very common in Blues but it is worth knowing them, as the bar chord shapes derived from them are used quite often. Here are three basic minor chord shapes. As with all previous chords, memorise each shape and then practice changing between them.

### Am

### Dm
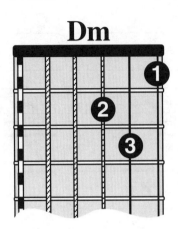

### Em

 **26.0**

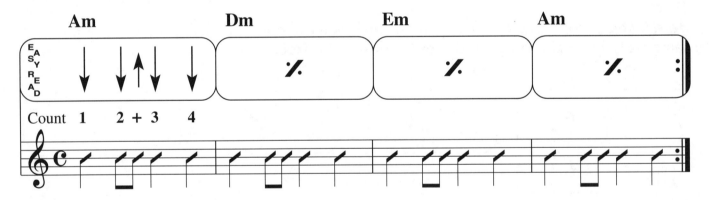

 **26.1**

In minor keys chords $\bar{I}$ and $\bar{IV}$ are usually minor. Chord $\bar{V}$ is sometimes minor and sometimes a 7th, as in this exercise in the key of E minor.

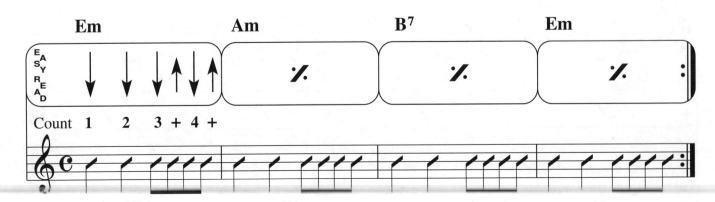

# Minor Bar Chords

Just as major chords can be altered to form 7ths, minor chords can be altered to form **minor 7ths.** Here are the shapes for the root 6 and root 5 minor bar chords and minor 7th bar chords.

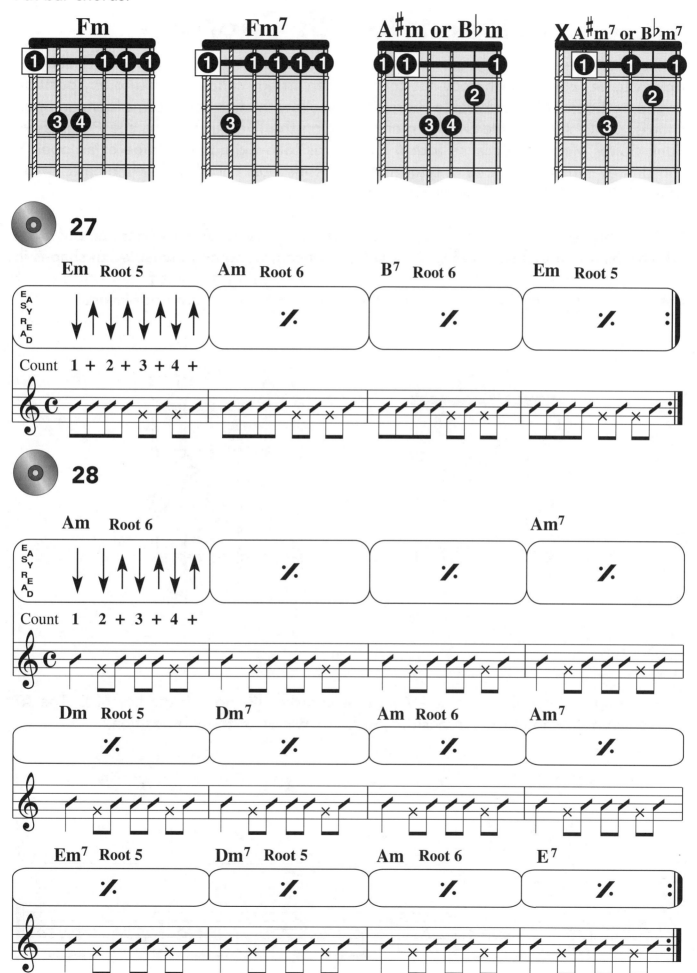

# LESSON FOURTEEN

## Moveable 7th Chords

Bar chords are probably the most common example of moveable chord shapes. However, any chord which does not contain open strings can be moved to any position on the fretboard. Most moveable chord shapes follow the five basic forms found in open chords, i.e. C, A, G, E and D. (For more detail on the five basic forms see *Progressive Funk Guitar Method*). Because root 6 bar chords follow the basic shape of an open E chord, they can be described as E form chords. Root 5 bar chords follow the basic shape of an A chord, so they can be described as A form chords.

It is possible to move other major chord shapes by the use of a first finger bar, but since 7th chords are more useful in Blues we will be concentrating on moveable 7th shapes in this lesson. A moveable D7 shape can be created by using the first finger on the root note on the 4th string. With this shape, the 5th and 6th strings are not played.

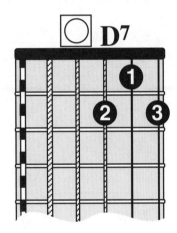

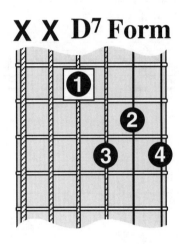

 **29**

This example uses the moveable D7 form as chords $\bar{I}$, $\bar{IV}$ and $\bar{V}$ in the key of E. The A7 chord can be found at the 7th position, while B7 will be at the 9th position.

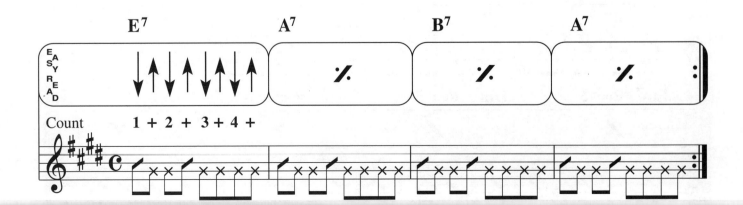

If you mute out the 1st and 6th strings, the basic C7 chord shape becomes moveable to any key. In this form the root note can be found on both the 5th and 2nd strings.

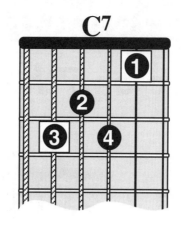

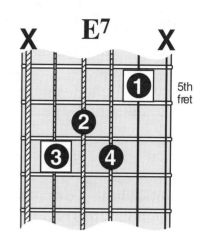

 **30**

Here is the last four bars of a Blues progression in the key of A, using the C7 form. Be careful with the change in rhythm in the fourth bar.

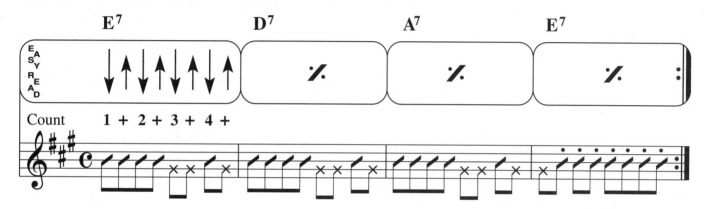

This next chord shape is a variation on the C7 form. The root note in this shape is on the 2nd string. Like the D7 form, this one uses only the first four strings.

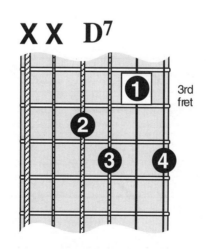

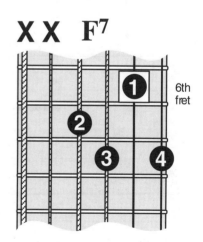

 **31**

Now try this progression using the alternate C7 form.

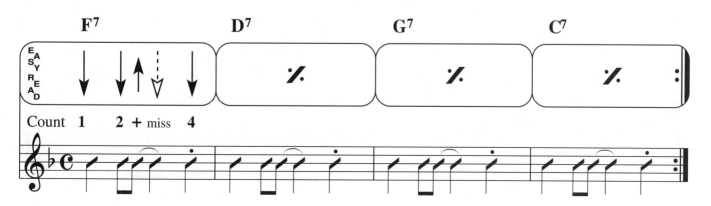

# LESSON FIFTEEN

## More on 7th Chords

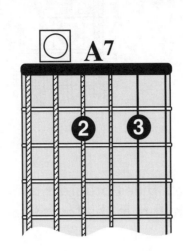

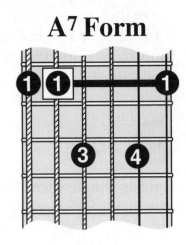

Continuing on with the moveable 7th shapes, here is an A7 form. This is a variation on the root 5 bar chord 7th. As with all A form chords, the root note is on the 5th string.

 **32**

Here is a 12 bar Blues in the key of C, using the moveable A7 form. Notice the use of the quick $\overline{IV}$ once again.

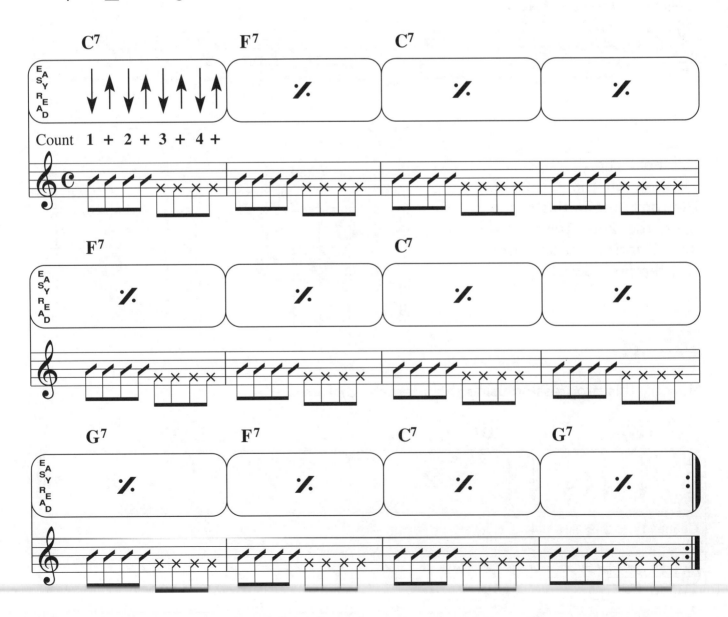

When using the G7 form as a moveable shape, it is common to use only the first four strings once again. This is partly because the full G7 bar chord shape is very awkward to move around the fretboard.

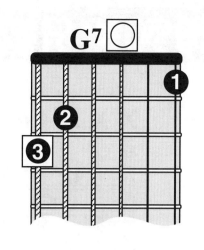

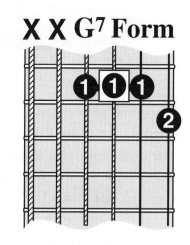

X X G7 Form

 **33**

This 12 bar Blues in the key of A uses only the G7 form moved up and down the fretboard. It also contains a new Blues technique, moving down one fret from a chord and then back to the original chord. This technique is often used to add colour and drive to the rhythm pattern.

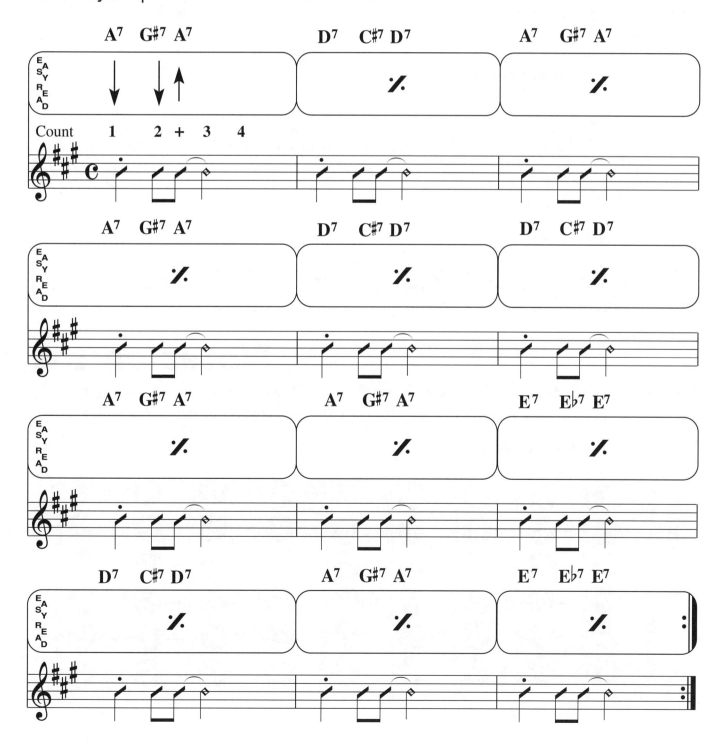

Here are two more useful 7th chord shapes. Both are derived from the E form and once again only the first four strings are used. The first shape has its root note on the first string, while the second one has root notes on both the first and fourth strings.

**X X E⁷ Form**

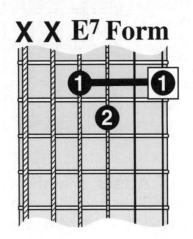

**X X E⁷ Form**

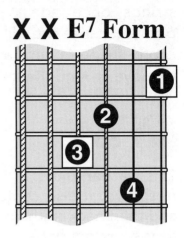

 **34**

This exercise alternates between these two shapes.

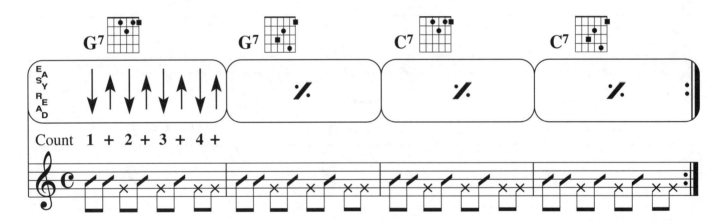

# Notes on the

Here is a fretboard diagram of all the notes on the guitar. Play the notes on each string from the the open 6th string is an **E** note and the note on the 12th fret of the 6th string is also an **E** note,

**1st String (Thinnest String)**

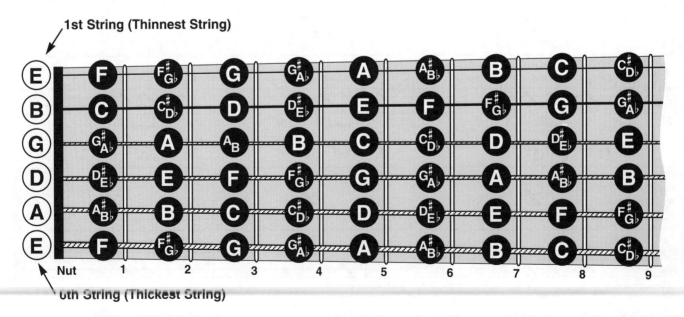

**6th String (Thickest String)**

# Learning the Notes

When using moveable chord shapes, it is important to be able to quickly find the correct fret at which to play each chord and also to be able to play equally well in all keys. The best way to achieve this is to memorise the names of all the notes on the fretboard. Blues uses many different chords which may take their name from any of the six strings, so be sure to learn all of the strings equally well.

Shown below is a diagram showing all the notes up to the 12th fret where they begin to repeat.

A good way to learn all the notes is to take one string at a time. Call the "in between" notes sharps as you progress up, and flats as you go back down. The dots on your guitar are good points of reference. You can use them to help the memorising process.

Next, pick the name of a note at random and find it as quickly as possible. When that becomes easy, move on to the next string.

Another good thing to do is to find the same note on every string. Usually a note appears twice on each string unless it is at the eleventh fret – except for guitars with 24 frets.

One last way to learn the notes is to go across each fret. Again use sharps as you go higher in pitch and flats as you go down.

# Guitar Fretboard

open notes to the 12th fret. The note on the 12th fret is one octave higher than the open note e.g. but is one octave higher.

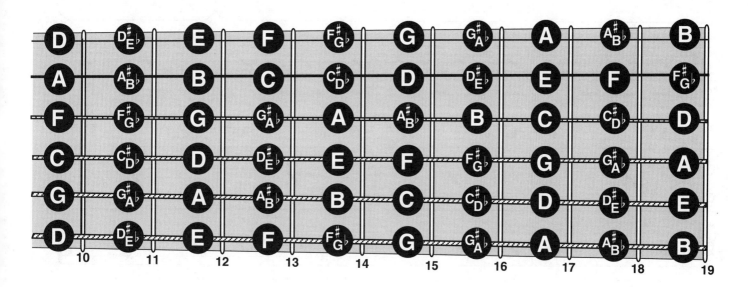

# LESSON SEVENTEEN

So far we have dealt with major chords and dominant 7th chords. Now comes another popular sound in Blues, the **Dominant 9th chord** (commonly called a 9th chord). A 9th chord is obtained by adding a major 3rd interval on top of a 7th chord. The chord will then contain the **1st, 3rd, 5th, ♭7th** and **9th** degrees of a major scale. Here is the most common voicing of the 9th chord. The third finger should clearly sound the 1st, 2nd and 3rd strings. The root note here is on the 5th string, under the second finger.

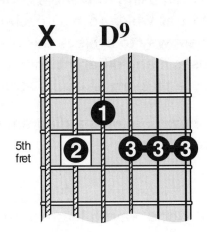

 **35**

Once you have the shape memorised, try this new 12 bar Blues which moves the 9th chord around the fretboard. In this exercise the shape is often moved briefly up or down one fret from chord Ī, ĪV or V̄. Listen to the effect it creates.

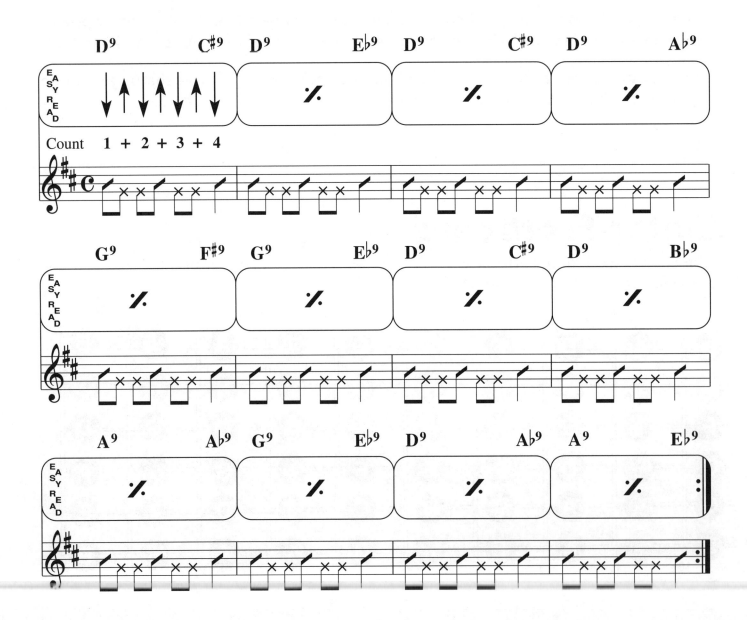

Here is another common 9th chord shape. This one can sometimes be difficult to locate correctly, since it doesn't contain the root note. The root can be found on the 6th string at the same fret as the third finger.

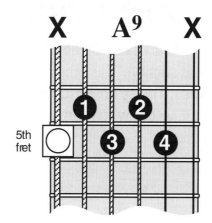

 **36**

Once you are comfortable with each of the 9th chord shapes, try playing a 12 bar Blues alternating between the two.

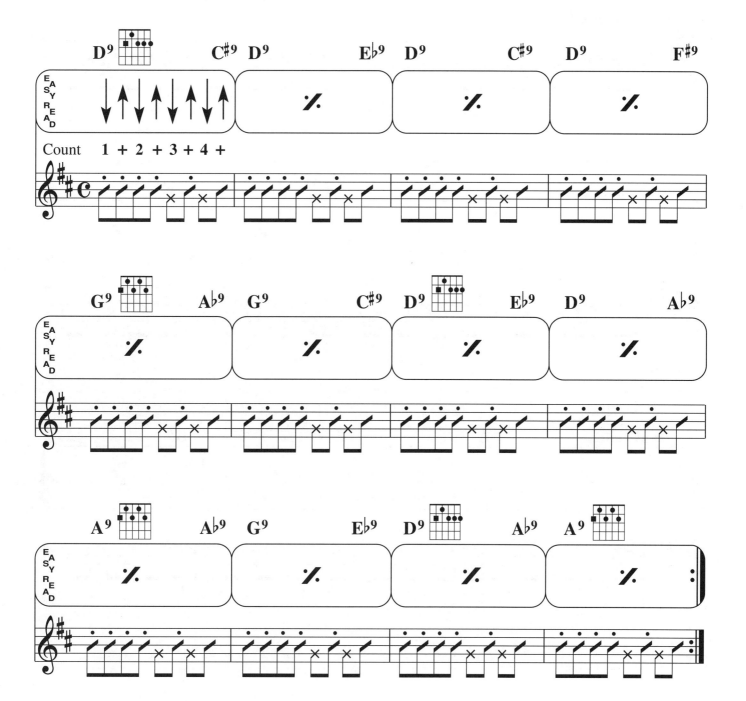

# 7th Chord Review

To finish things off, here is a 12 bar Blues progression making use of many of the moveable 7th chords introduced in this section. This progression moves all over the fretboard to really test your knowledge of the shapes. The strumming pattern here is quite difficult. Practice it slowly on one chord before applying it to the whole progression.

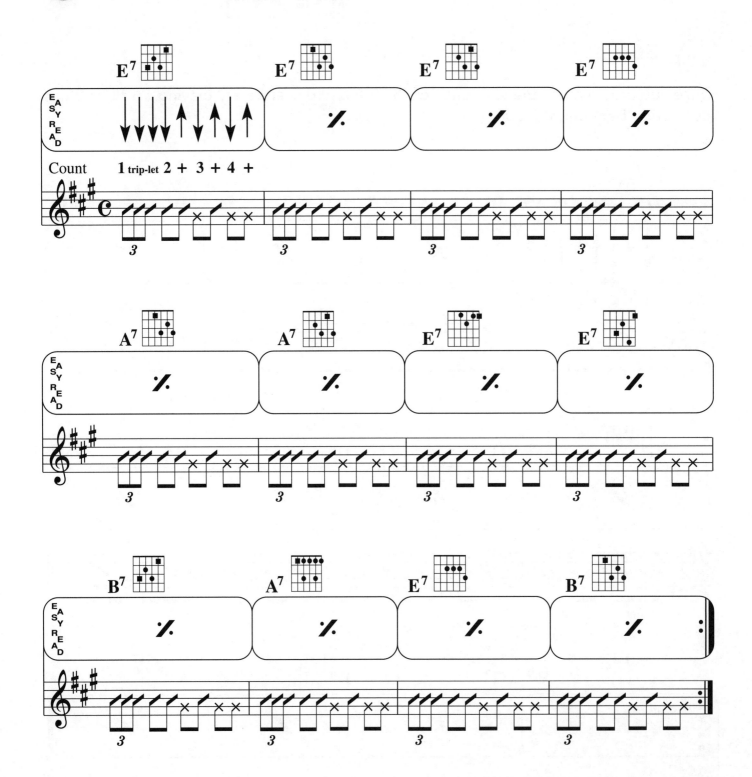

# SECTION 3

# Single Note Riffs, Boogie Rhythms

# LESSON EIGHTEEN

## The Pentatonic Scale

Not all Blues rhythm guitar parts use chords, many songs sound great with single note riffs instead, often doubling or complementing the bass line. To create good riffs, it is necessary to know several scales and arpeggios. Probably the most common scale in Blues is the **minor pentatonic scale**. As the name suggests, this scale contains five different notes. Its degrees compared to a major scale are **1**, ♭**3**, **4**, **5**, and ♭**7**. Here is a common fingering for the minor pentatonic scale in the key of A.

### A Minor Pentatonic

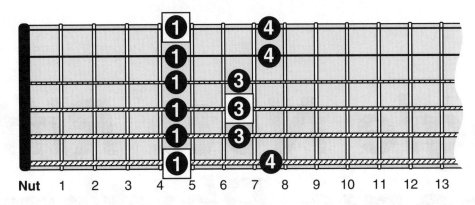

Try running up and down the scale a few times until you have the sound and the fingering memorised. Here are two examples showing the scale ascending and descending.

**38.0**

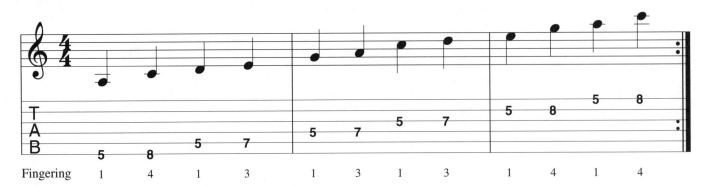

**38.1**

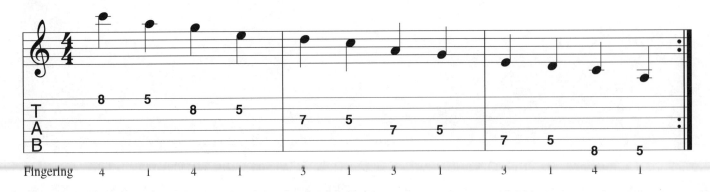

**39**

Most single note riffs which follow the 12 bar Blues progression begin on degrees 1, 4 and 5 of whichever scale they are using. The term **"riff"** means a short repeating phrase. The more familiar you are with these scale degrees, the easier it will be to learn new riffs. This exercise should help you become familiar with the positioning of degrees 1, 4 and 5 within the minor pentatonic scale.

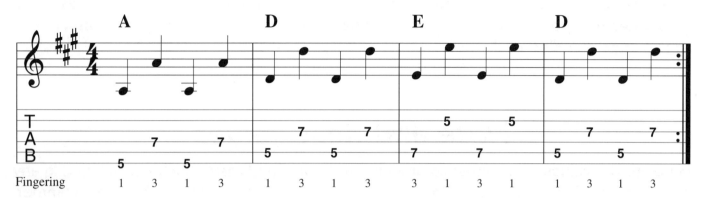

**40**

In many riffs, the fingering for the 5th degree of the scale is on the same strings as the 4th degree, but moved up two frets. This ends up more practical than changing to a different set of strings. The new fingering is demonstrated in bars nine and twelve of this exercise. The picking here should be alternating down and upstrokes.

# LESSON NINETEEN

## Rhythm Notation

It is a good idea to learn how to read rhythms even if you don't read music. Everybody uses the same notes, but it is the control of rhythm and phrasing which to a large extent separates the great players from the average. The very term "rhythm guitar" assumes a good understanding of rhythms.

## Note and Rest Values

Here are the values of the most commonly used notes and rests which you will find in any style of music. The note values shown here are related to $\frac{4}{4}$ time which is the most common time signature in Blues.

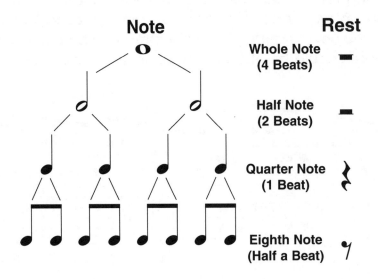

## Dotted Notes

A dot placed directly after a note increases its value by one half, as shown below.

# The Shuffle

One of the most common rhythms in Blues is called a **shuffle**. The term shuffle describes the type of rhythm. The shuffle rhythm is based on eighth note triplets (three notes per beat).

 **41.0**

Here is a bar of eighth note triplets.

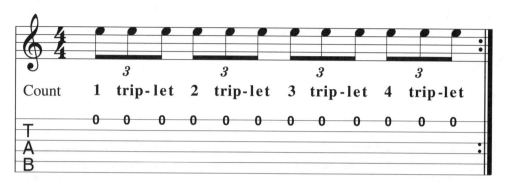

Remember that there is a different sound for each part of the triplet: **one-trip-let**, this is because there could be a rest on any part of the triplet, and you need to know where you are exactly.

 **41.1**

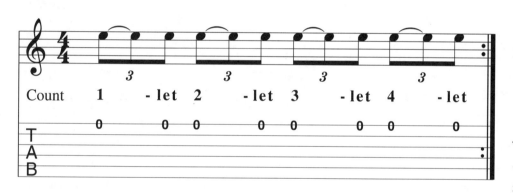

In a shuffle, the middle note of the triplet is not played but is tied to the first note. This is also called **swinging** the 8th notes. Notice that the "trip" is not played. The term "shuffle" means a continuous stream of swing 8th notes.

It is also possible to write a shuffle in ordinary 8th notes and indicate that they are to be interpreted as a shuffle by writing "swing 8ths" or "shuffle" or the symbol shown below at the start of example 42. In this example, the all notes are swung.

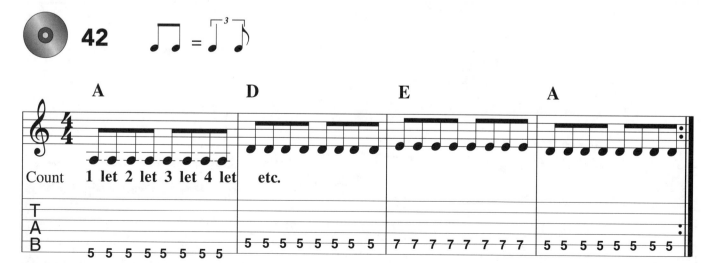

# LESSON TWENTY

## Shuffle Riffs, Ties

Now let's put the shuffle rhythm to good use. Here is a 12 bar Blues shuffle riff. Notice how all of the notes which fall on the beat are played staccato. This is very common when playing shuffles. The last bar in this exercise departs from the riff and used triplets instead, which helps to build momentum leading up to the repeat.

# The Tie

A tie is a method of increasing the time value of a note. It is indicated by a curved line connecting two consecutive notes of the same pitch. Ties are commonly used to create syncopated rhythms, as demonstrated in the following example.

 **44**

In the first bar all the written notes are played, while in the second bar the fourth 8th note is tied to the following note. The difference should be easy to hear.

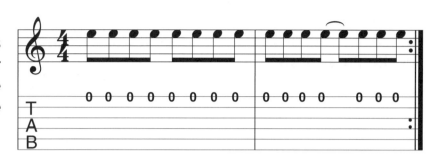

 **45**

Here is a riff using the rhythm from bar two of the previous example.

# LESSON TWENTY ONE

## The Blues Scale

It is possible to add extra notes to the minor pentatonic scale. The most common addition is the flattened 5th degree. Once this note is added, it becomes what is known as the **Blues Scale**.

| A minor pentatonic | A | C | D | E | G |
| --- | --- | --- | --- | --- | --- |
| | 1 | ♭3 | 4 | 5 | ♭7 |

| A Blues scale | A | C | D | E♭ | E | G |
| --- | --- | --- | --- | --- | --- | --- |
| | 1 | ♭3 | 4 | ♭5 | 5 | ♭7 |

Here is a common moveable fingering of the Blues scale in the key of A.

## A Blues Scale

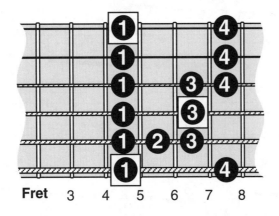

Fret   3   4   5   6   7   8

🔘 **46**

Run through the fingering until you are comfortable with it and can play it from memory.

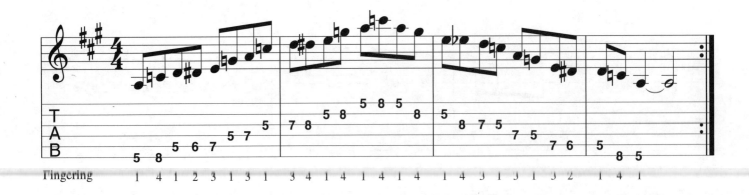

Now try this 12 bar Blues riff which makes use of the Blues scale. Once again the rhythm contains ties, this time with a triplet at the end of each bar. Practice it slowly at first and take care with the rhythm. In Blues, the rhythm is just as important as which notes you play.

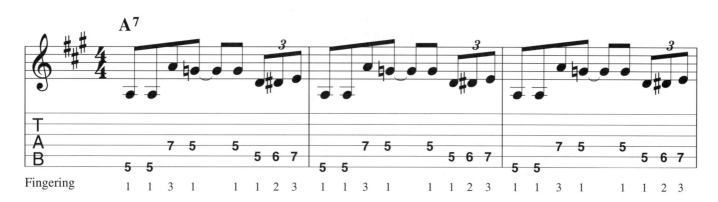

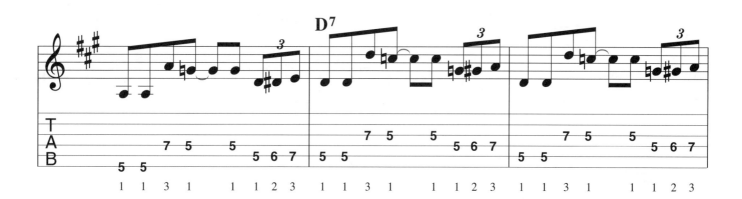

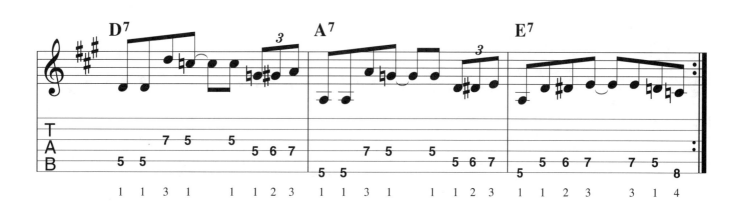

# LESSON TWENTY TWO

## The Mixolydian Scale

Another interesting sound used to create Blues riffs is the **Mixolydian** scale, or mode. Its degrees are **1**, **2**, **3**, **4**, **5**, **6**, and ♭**7**. Here it is in the key of A.

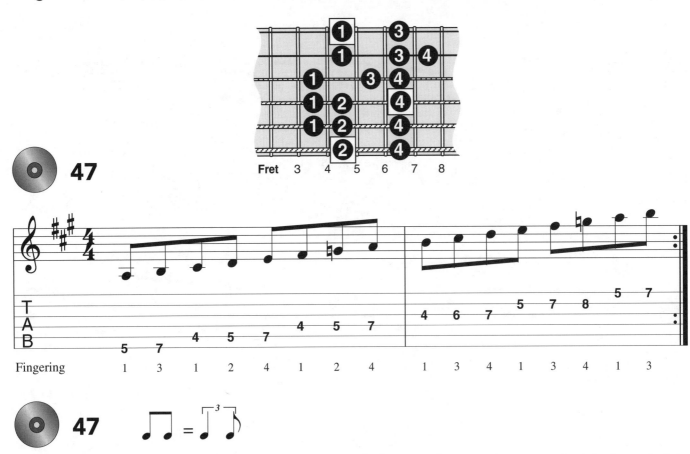

**47**

Fingering: 1 3 1 2 4 1 2 4    1 3 4 1 3 4 1 3

**47**

Here is a 12 bar Blues riff based on the mixolydian scale. You have probably heard this one many times.

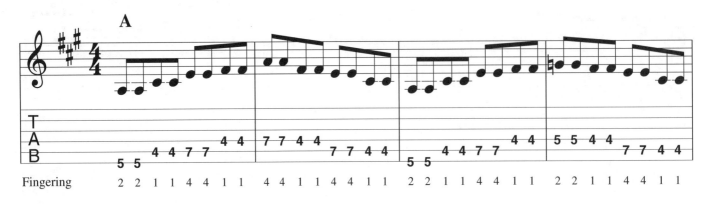

Fingering: 2 2 1 1 4 4 1 1   4 4 1 1 4 4 1 1   2 2 1 1 4 4 1 1   2 2 1 1 4 4 1 1

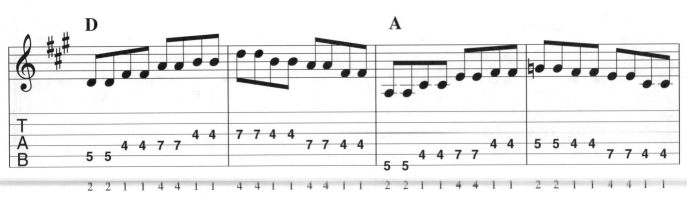

2 2 1 1 4 4 1 1   4 4 1 1 4 4 1 1   2 2 1 1 4 4 1 1   2 2 1 1 4 4 1 1

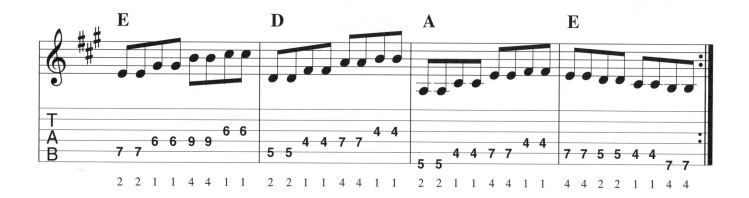

**50**

Observe the fingering carefully in this exercise and once again pay special attention to the rhythm.

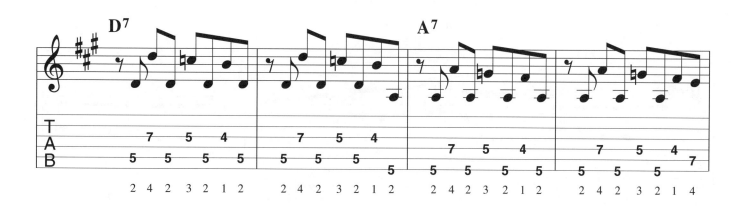

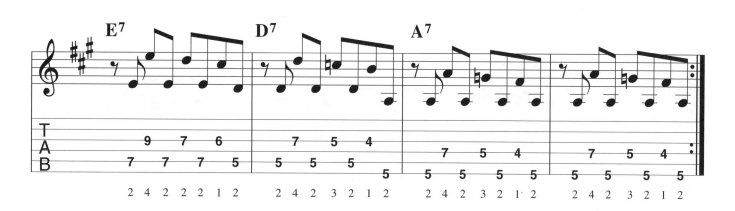

# LESSON TWENTY THREE

## Open String Riffs

All of the riffs studied so far have used moveable fingerings which enable you to play them in any key. However, there are many riffs which make use of open strings, particularly in the keys of A and E. Here is the riff from Example 49, this time played in the second position and making use of the open strings.

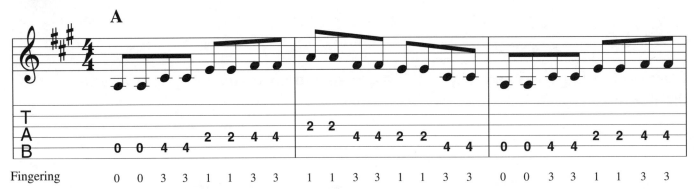

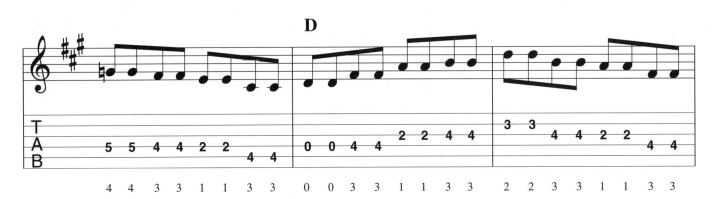

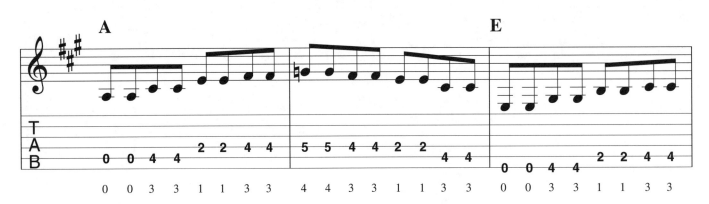

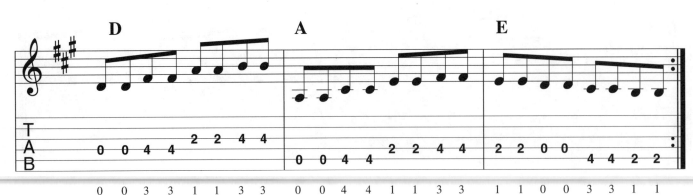

**52**

Here is the same riff in the key of E, with a slight variation at the end. Try creating some of your own riffs making use of the open strings.

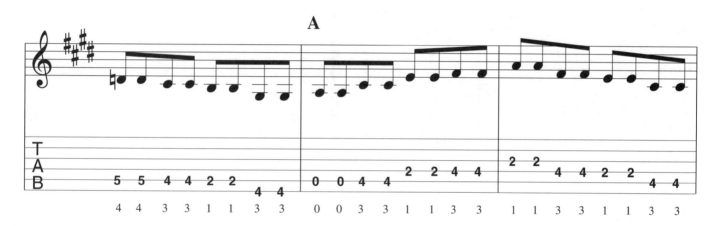

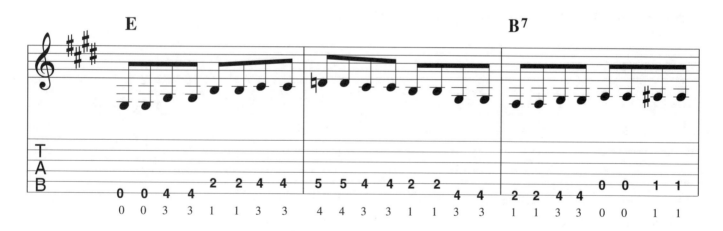

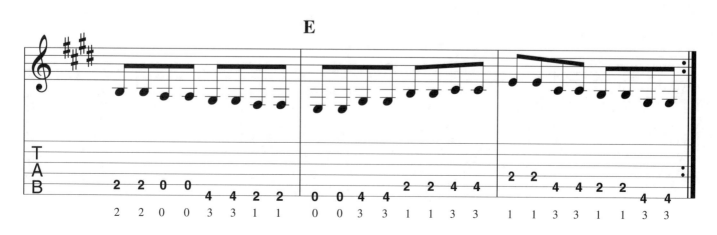

# LESSON TWENTY FOUR

## Rests

Whatever the style of music, the notes you don't play are as significant as the ones you do play. An important element in Blues is the use of space between the notes or chords. The use of rests is the most common way of creating space between notes or chords. To refresh your memory on the ways in which rests are written and their various values, go back and look at the note values chart in Lesson 20. Although two beat and four beat rests are used, one beat and half beat rests are much more common. Here are some exercises using these rests. This first one uses the quarter note or one beat rest.

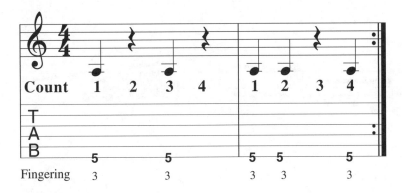

Now try this 12 bar Blues using the rhythm of the previous example.

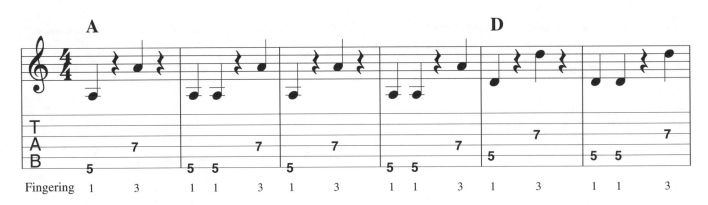

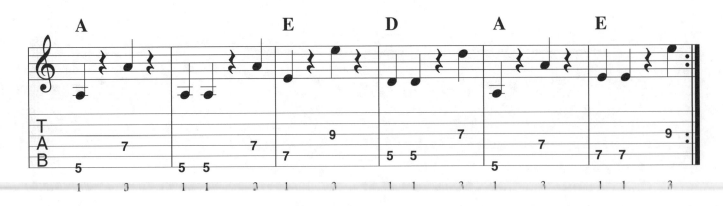

# Eighth Note Rests

Eighth note rests are very important in Boogie rhythms, which will be the subject of the next lesson. The eighth notes in these next exercises are swung. Be sure to count and tap your foot as you play.

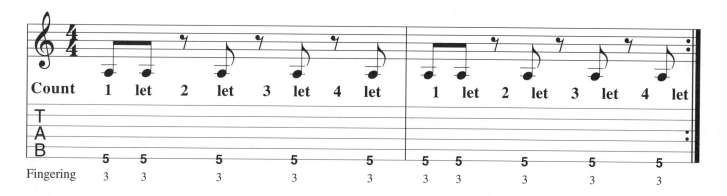

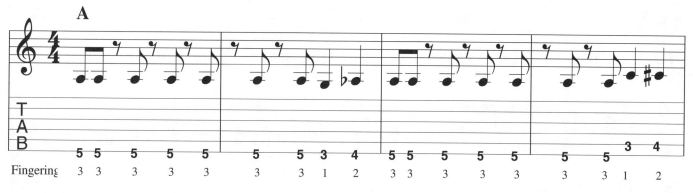

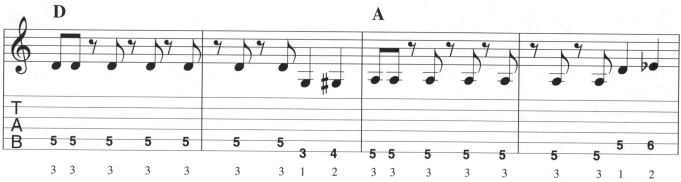

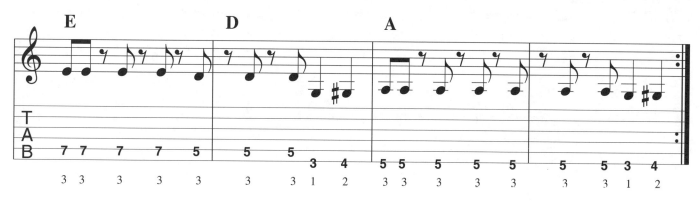

# LESSON TWENTY FIVE

## Boogie Rhythms

A Boogie is a particular type of shuffle which often makes use of rests and percussive strumming on the beat to help drive the rhythm along. Boogie songs often stay on one chord rather than following a 12 bar pattern. The artists best known for this style are John Lee Hooker and ZZ Top. Example 57 is a basic boogie rhythm.

**57**

**58**

Here's a slight variation, this time using percussive strums in place of the rests.

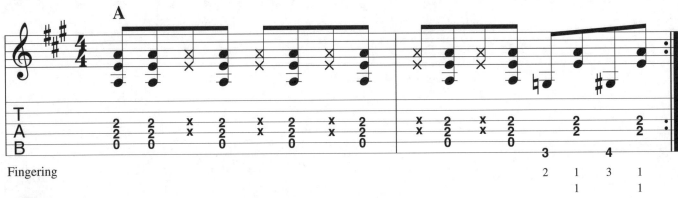

**59**

Now try this variation.

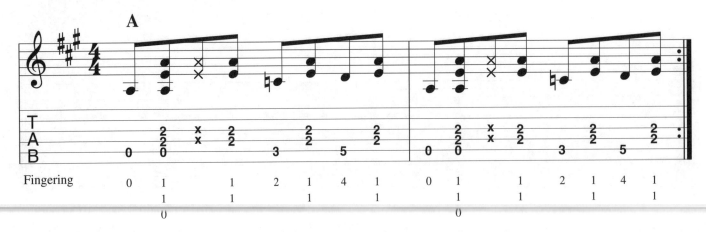

Here are two more variations, followed by an eight bar boogie solo.

To end this section, here is another well known 12 bar Blues riff in the key of A. To get the right sound on the double note in this riff it will be necessary to pull downwards with the first finger to bend the notes slightly. (For more on slight bends see *Progressive Blues Lead Guitar Method*.)

 **63**

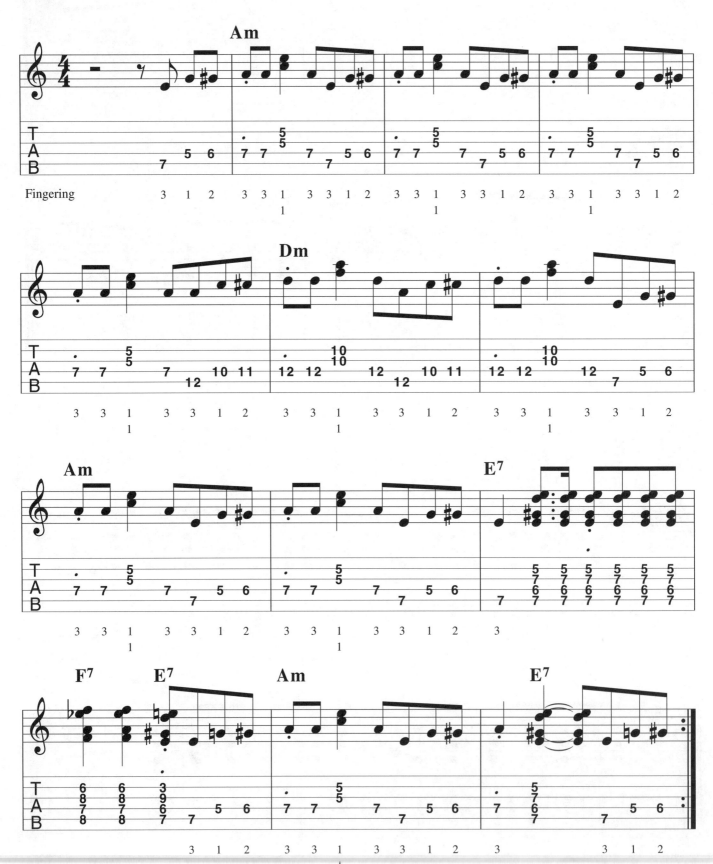

# SECTION 4

## Shuffles, Turnarounds

# LESSON TWENTY SIX

## Two Note Chords

Probably the most common sound in Blues rhythm guitar is the shuffle rhythm played on two strings. This rhythm pattern uses what are commonly called **fifth chords**, or **power chords**. Technically a chord requires three or more notes, but as these two note fingerings are now commonly used in several styles of music it has become acceptable to refer to them as chords. Three popular fifth chords in the open position are A5, D5 and E5, which can work together as chords $\bar{I}$, $\bar{IV}$ and $\bar{V}$ in the key of A.

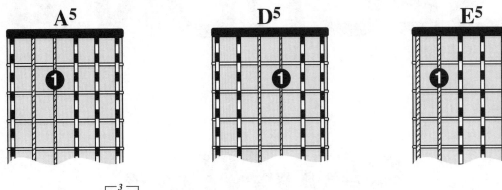

**64**

Practice changing between these chords until you can play them smoothly and in time. Notice the use of the shuffle rhythm. Use all downstrokes when playing this style.

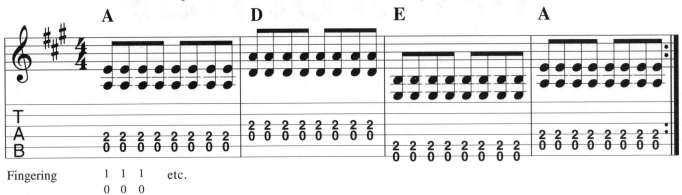

To complete the pattern for the classic shuffle sound, the third finger is placed two frets up the neck on the same string as the first finger. The same two strings are played as in the fifth chord. Keep the first finger down even when playing with the third finger. This will result in a smoother, more solid sound.

**65**

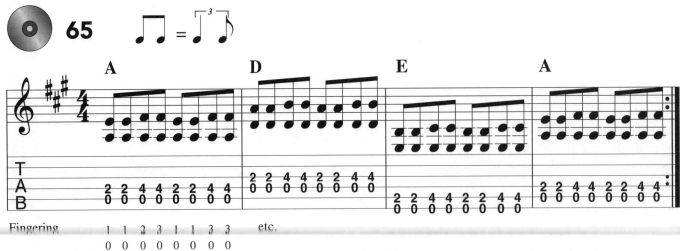

When playing this type of shuffle, it is common to damp the strings slightly with the right hand. This results in a tighter, more chunky sound. Rest the heel of the hand on the strings at the bridge and then pick the strings you want to sound. It may take a bit of practice to get the desired sound, it all depends on the exact position of the right hand and the amount of pressure used on the strings. Here is an example.

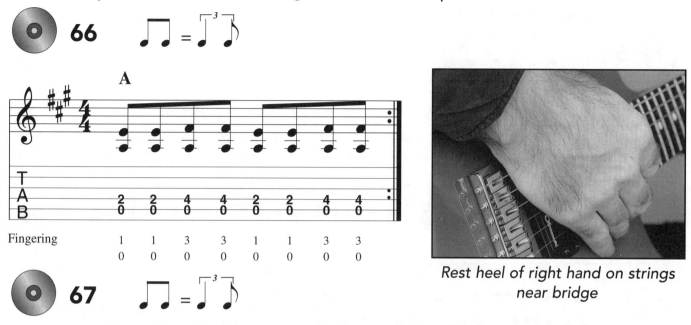

*Rest heel of right hand on strings near bridge*

Now try applying the right hand damping technique to this 12 bar Blues.

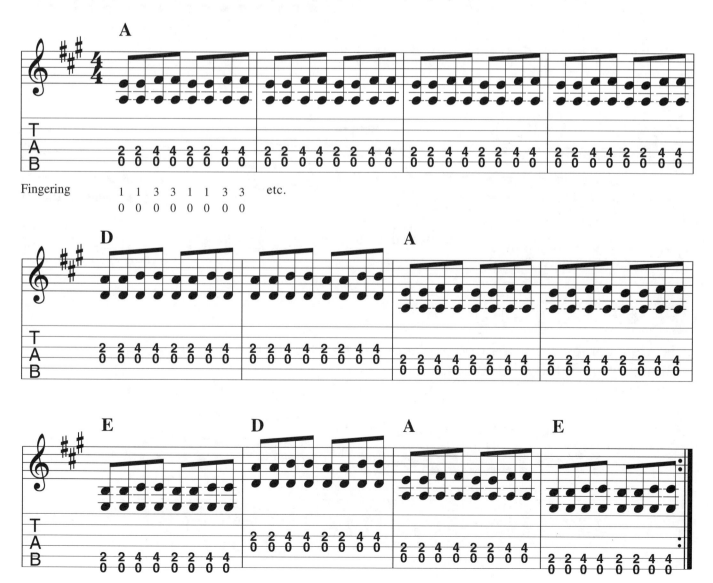

# LESSON TWENTY SEVEN

## Shuffle Variations

Here are some variations on the basic shuffle pattern. This next one requires the use of the fourth finger at the fifth fret.

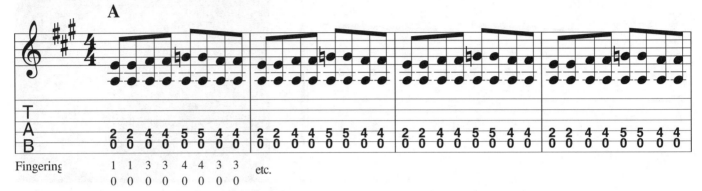

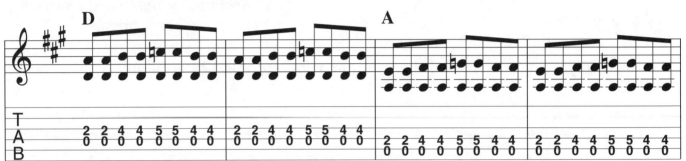

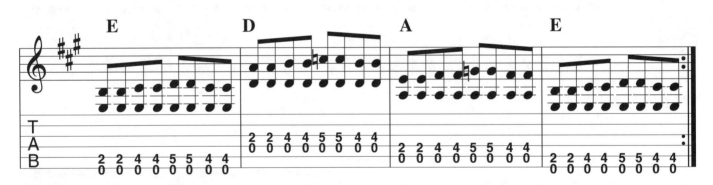

This idea comes from a boogie piano left hand pattern. The progression here is a common form of the 8 bar Blues.

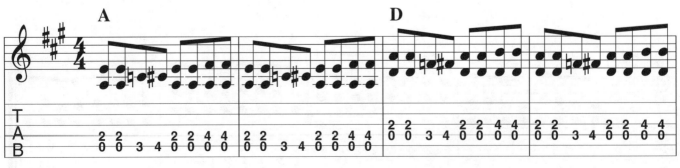

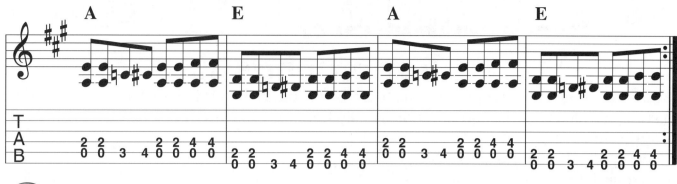

**70**

Here the new notes from the previous two exercises are combined in a single note riff style. The final two bars of this exercise depart from the riff and introduce a new phrase which ends on an E7 chord. This is called a **turnaround.**

# LESSON TWENTY EIGHT

## Turnarounds

A turnaround is a two bar phrase which can be found at the end of each verse in the vast majority of Blues songs. Turnarounds usually begin on chord $\underline{I}$ in bar eleven of a 12 bar progression and move to chord $\underline{V}$ in bar twelve. A turnaround has the effect of finishing a verse while setting the progression up for the start of the next verse. Here is an example of a turnaround, first by itself and then at the end of a 12 bar progression.

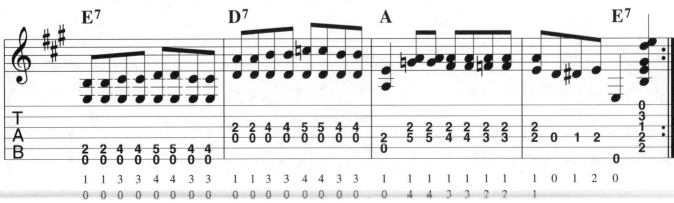

This is a variation on the previous turnaround. Instead of playing two notes together, the same notes are played consecutively, alternating between the third and fourth strings.

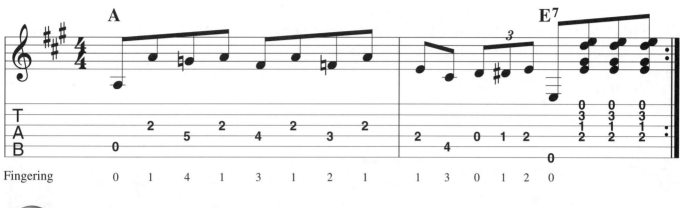

Now listen to the effect when the turnaround is added to a 12 bar Blues progression.

# LESSON TWENTY NINE

## *More on Turnarounds*

Here are several more turnarounds to give you some new ideas. Any of these turnarounds can be used at the end of a 12 bar Blues progression. Often the choice of turnaround depends on the song and what the other instruments are playing. It is always useful to have a collection of turnarounds up your sleeve.

**75**

**76**

Keep the little finger on the A note on the first string while changing notes on the second string.

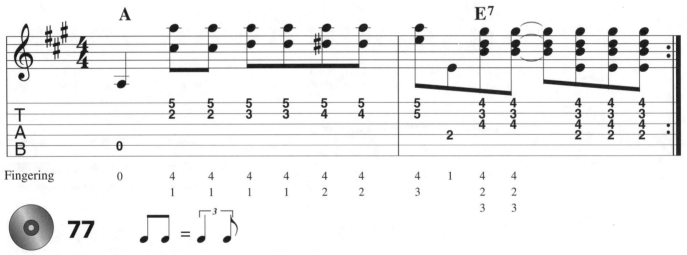

**77**

This variation on the previous turnaround ends on an E9 chord.

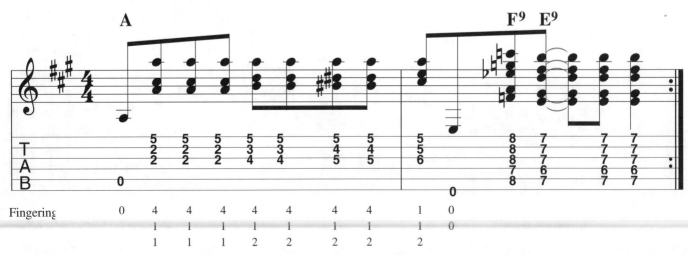

These next two turnarounds end on different shapes of the E7 chord. Now you have the basic idea of how turnarounds work, try creating some of your own. Listen to Blues albums for more ideas, each player will have a slightly different approach to turnarounds.

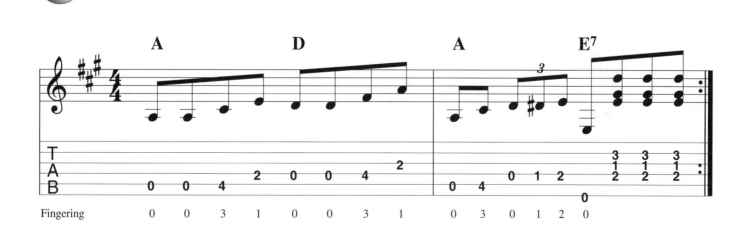

# LESSON THIRTY

## Moveable Shuffle Patterns

All the shuffle patterns in the previous few lessons have involved the use of open strings, making them unsuitable for moving up and down the fretboard. However, there are other patterns not including open strings, which can easily be moved to any position on the fretboard.

**81**

Here once again is the basic shuffle in the key of A, this time played in the fifth position. The first and third fingers remain on the strings, while the fourth finger stretches up two frets on the same string as the third finger.

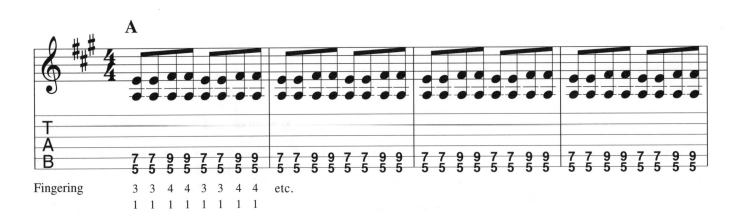

Fingering
3 3 4 4 3 3 4 4   etc.
1 1 1 1 1 1 1 1

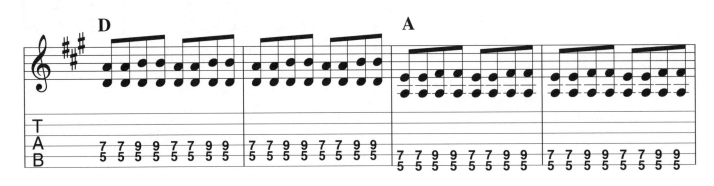

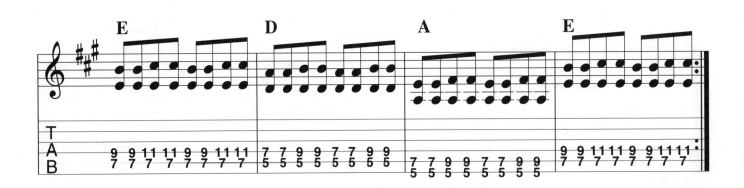

**82**

As with the patterns using open strings, a turnaround can be added to any moveable fingering. This turnaround is identical to the one used in Example 74, but the fingering has been changed. This now becomes a moveable turnaround.

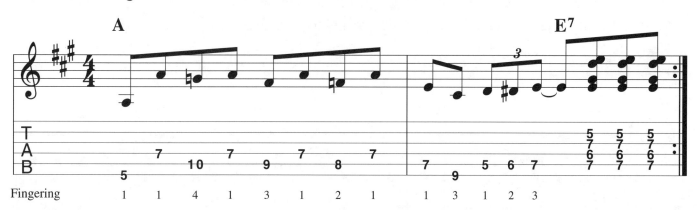

**83**

Here is the turnaround applied to the 12 bar Blues progression.

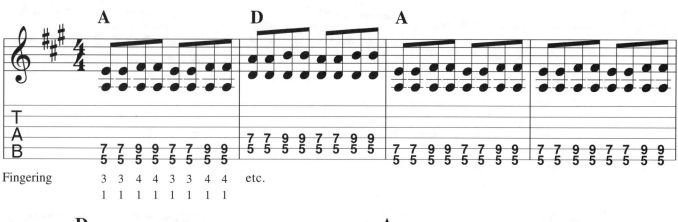

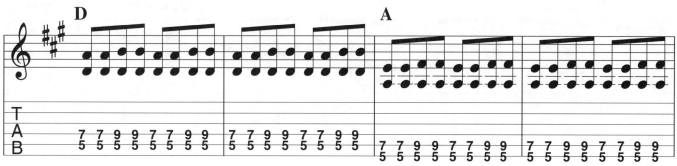

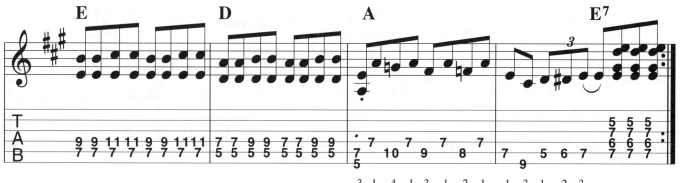

# LESSON THIRTY ONE

## Moveable Shuffle Variations

Here are two more moveable shuffle patterns. The second one is a variation on the first. Each one has a different turnaround. In both these exercises the first finger bars the 6th, 5th and 4th strings before moving to the 5th, 4th and 3rd strings.

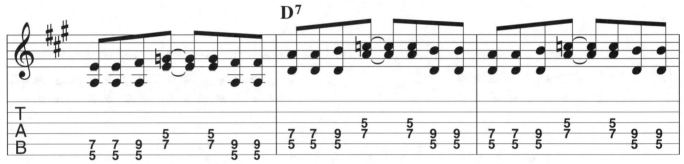

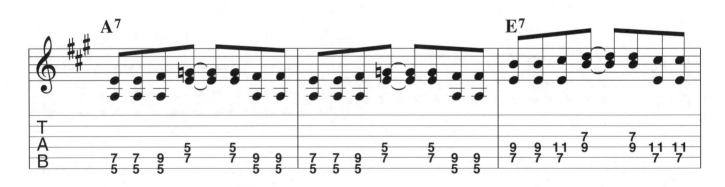

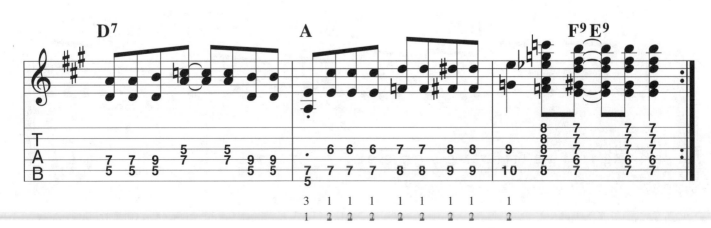

**85**

The turnaround in this exercise should sound familiar. It is one of the classic Blues sounds.

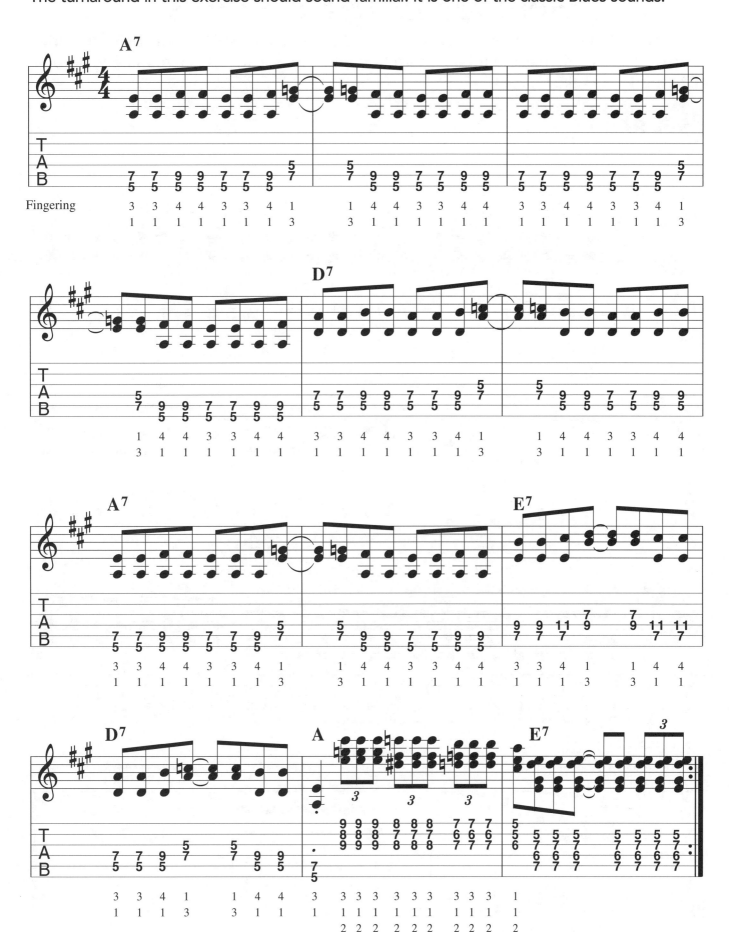

# LESSON THIRTY TWO

## Shuffles in The Key of E

E is one of the most common keys for Blues. Once again, much use is made of the open strings. Here is the basic shuffle pattern in the key of E, with a turnaround ending on a B7 chord in the final bar.

**86**

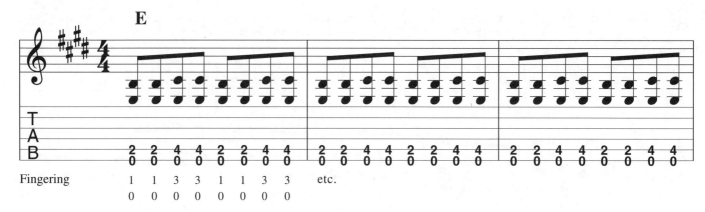

Fingering

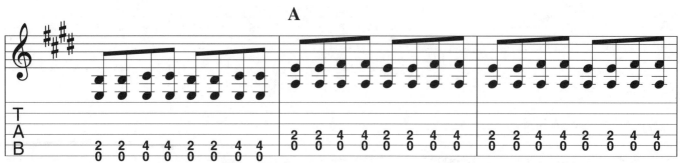

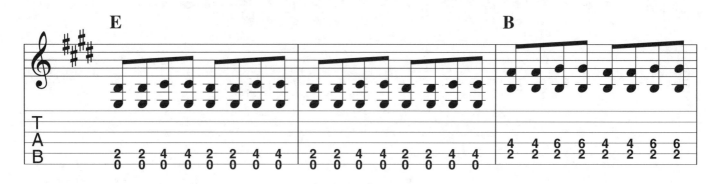

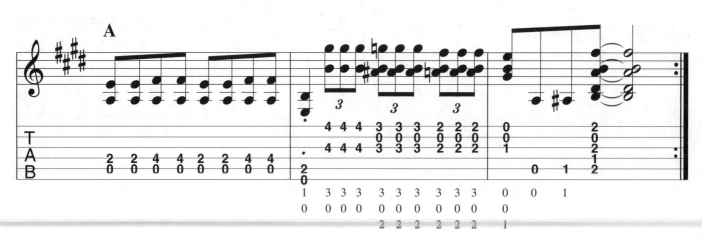

This variation uses one of the earlier turnarounds transposed to the key of E. It also contains a chromatic run between chords Ī and ĪV, using fifth chords. Also watch for the extra stretch with the little finger in bar 6. This may take some time to master, so take it slowly at first.

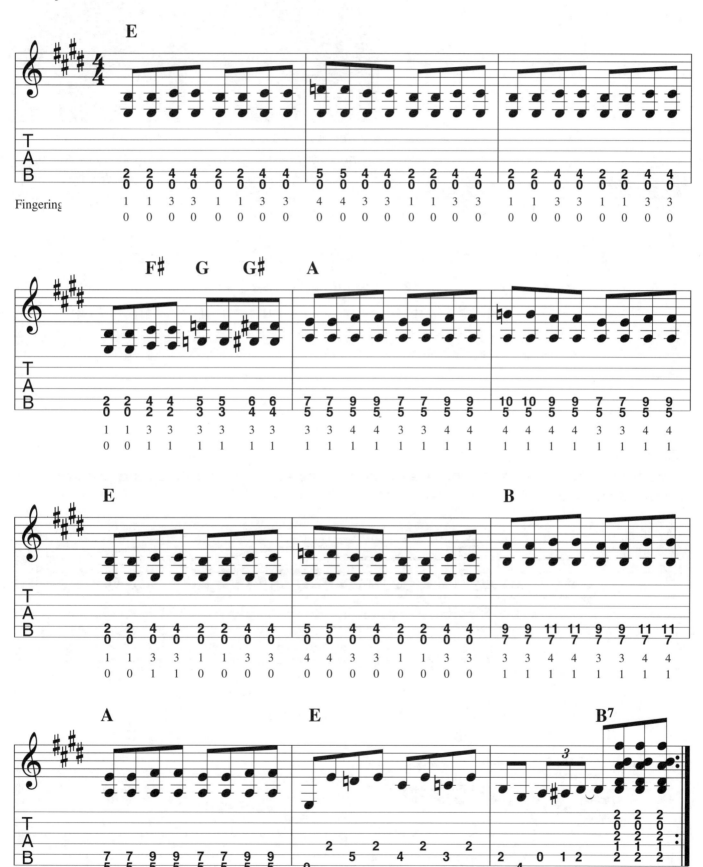

# The Hammer-On

A hammer on is executed by picking a note and then hammering a left hand finger onto the string. The hammer-on is indicated by a curved line and the symbol **H**.

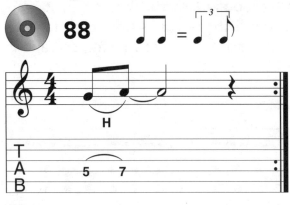

*Begin by playing the note on the fifth fret, fourth string.*

*Hammer third finger onto seventh fret of fourth string.*

This exercise should help you gain control of hammer-ons.

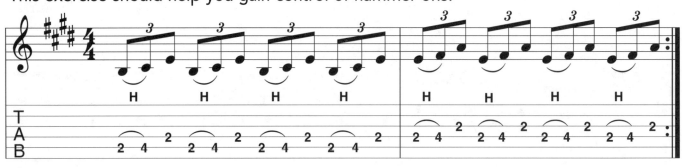

Now try this 8 bar Blues making use of the hammer-on. Take care with the position shift on the B chord in bar 6.

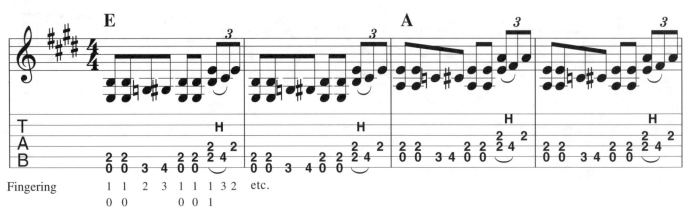

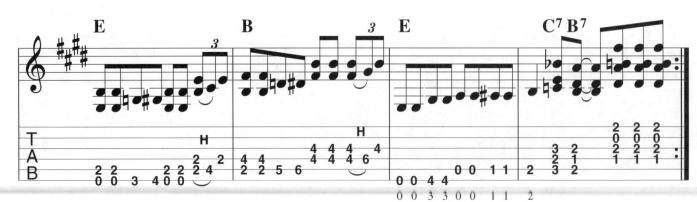

Here is another interesting shuffle in E, making use of harmony notes.

# LESSON THIRTY THREE

Another effective method of playing a shuffle is to rock backwards and forwards between an E chord shape and an A chord shape. Here is an exercise to help you gain control of this technique.

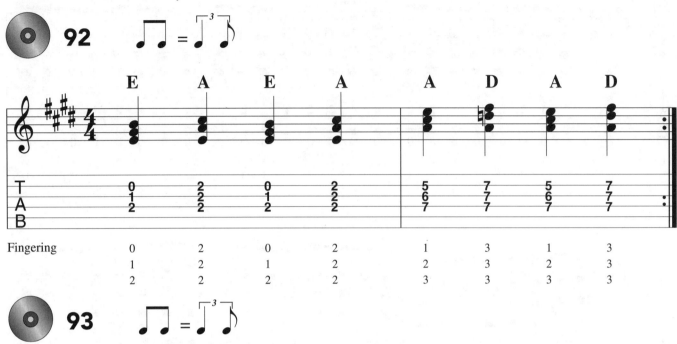

Here is the technique applied to a 12 bar Blues shuffle.

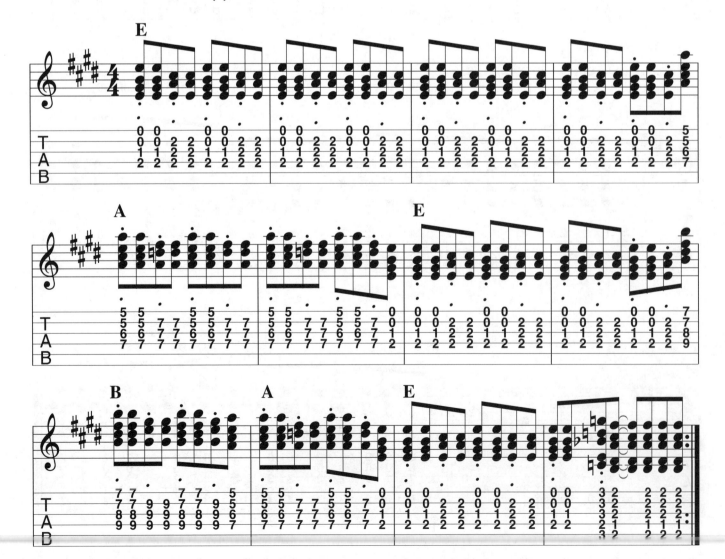

This example uses a variation on the rocking technique. Take care with the top note of each of the chords here. Sometimes the highest note is on the first string, other times it is on the second string. This one also contains a chromatic run between chords Ī and ĪV̄.

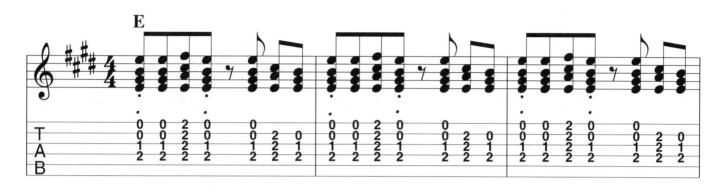

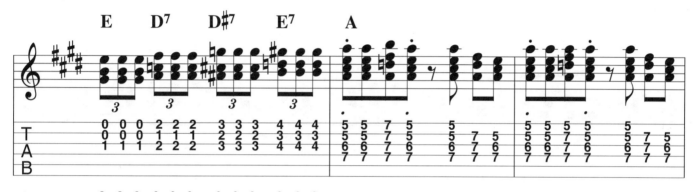

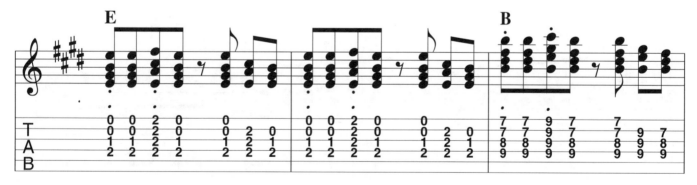

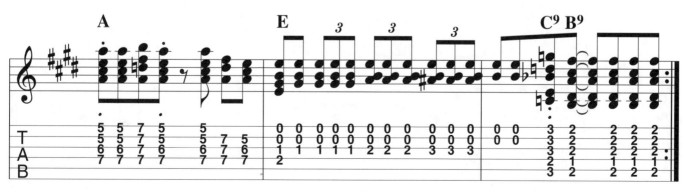

# LESSON THIRTY FOUR

Here is one more way of playing a shuffle. This one involves mainly the 2nd, 3rd and 4th strings.

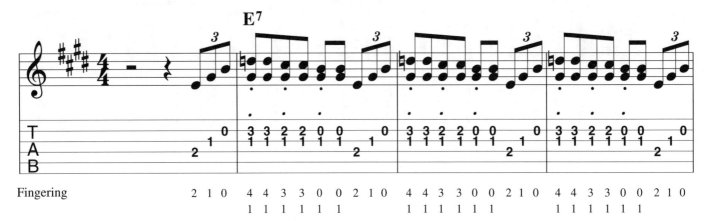

Fingering

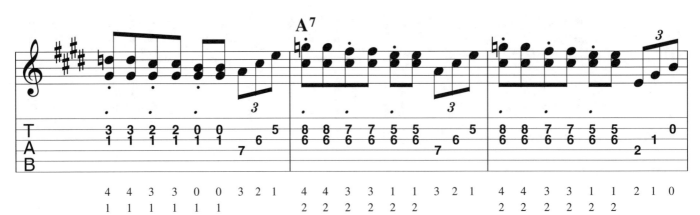

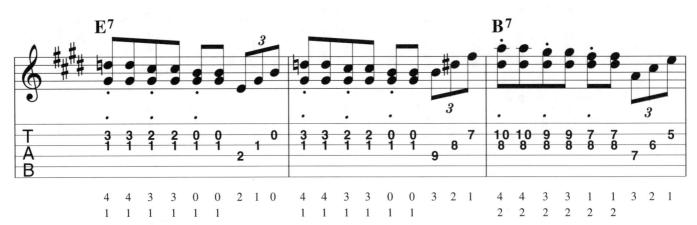

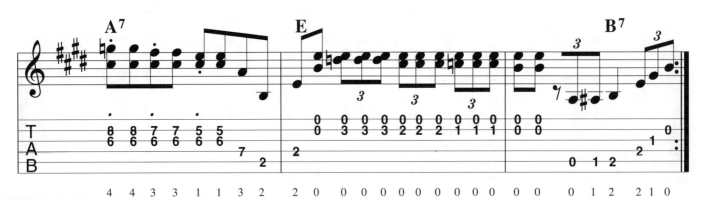

If you've got this far, your rhythm playing should be sounding very good. One of the best things about being a good rhythm guitarist is that lots of people will want to play with you, since most guitarists just want to play lead and often neglect developing their rhythm skills.

Here is a variation on the previous shuffle, this time in the key of A. The first finger is used to cover each of the first three strings for much of this progression.

## PROGRESSIVE BLUES LEAD GUITAR METHOD
### FOR BEGINNER TO ADVANCED
This book takes a unique approach to learning Blues lead guitar. The most common scale used in Blues – the minor pentatonic scale, is used immediately to make music. The scale is learned in five basic positions which cover the whole fretboard, along with a variety of licks and solos demonstrating all the important techniques such as slides, vibrato and note bending, as used by all the great Blues players.

## PROGRESSIVE BLUES LEAD GUITAR TECHNIQUE
### INTERMEDIATE TO ADVANCED
The central approach of this book is the development of musical technique, dealing with rhythm as it applies to lead guitar playing and concentrating on the development of phrasing and timing and how to really get the most out of the notes you play. Along the way, the book introduces the Blues scale and other important scales and arpeggios commonly used by Blues players. Also contains lots of great solos.

## PROGRESSIVE BLUES GUITAR LICKS
### FOR BEGINNER TO ADVANCED
Packed full of Blues guitar licks and solos incorporating styles and techniques used by the world's greatest Blues players. Includes sections on turnarounds, intro's and endings, call and response, dynamics and learning from other instruments. The licks cover a variety of styles such as shuffles, traditional slow Blues, Boogie, Jazz style Blues and R&B and Funk grooves. Also includes examples demonstrating how different licks can be put together to form whole solos, opening up endless possibilities for improvisation.

## PROGRESSIVE BLUES GUITAR SOLOS
### INTERMEDIATE TO ADVANCED
Contains a great selection of Blues solos in a variety of styles reflecting the whole history of the Blues tradition from early Delta Blues to contemporary Blues Rock. Demonstrates various methods of creating solos along with sections on vocal style phrasing, call and response, developing a theme, dynamics and the use of space. Many of the solos are written in the styles of Blues legends like Muddy Waters, John Lee Hooker, BB, Albert and Freddy King, Buddy Guy, Albert Collins, Peter Green, Magic Sam, Otis Rush, Eric Clapton and Stevie Ray Vaughan.

## PROGRESSIVE BLUES ACOUSTIC GUITAR METHOD
### FOR BEGINNING BLUES GUITARISTS
Covers all the important aspects of Acoustic Blues Guitar. This book introduces popular Blues progressions, Blues Rhythms, Basic Blues Lead Guitar Patterns and Lead Guitar Techniques. You will learn how to combine Blues rhythms and Blues licks, fingerpicking Blues styles such as the Constant Bass Line style and the Alternating Thumb style and an introduction to Acoustic Slide guitar.